DRUMMER'S POLYMETRIC MASTERY

Cross-Rhythmic Grooves for the Creative Mind

by Jason Gianni

Executive Producer: Rob Wallis

Edited by Joe Bergamini

Music Engraving: Jason Gianni

Cover Art: Jody Gianni

Book Layout: Terry Branam

VIDEO FILES: DOWNLOAD or STREAM
To access the video content that comes with this book, go to:
https://www.halleonard.com/mylibrary
Enter code: **1678-1547-7827-7643**

HUDSON MUSIC

www.hudsonmusic.com

CONTENTS

CONTENTS

INTRODUCTION

As far back as I can remember, I was drawn to music that contained "more." More of everything: more harmonic & melodic structure, more length to the songs, more imaginative or even unconventional type of playing, and generally just more substance or intent to the songwriting. I was initially too young & inexperienced to analyze the details of what I was hearing and what attracted me to my listening choices. However, as my percussion journey progressed and my education in music analysis evolved, I was able to define those very characteristics that piqued my interests. The odd or mixed meters of Rush, Kansas, Gentle Giant, the Mahavishnu Orchestra and Jeff Beck, to the epic conceptual pieces or albums from Yes, Genesis, Jethro Tull, Frank Zappa, Marillion, Miles Davis, Mussorgsky, Beethoven, Mahler and Messiaen, and to the multi-layered vocal harmonies of the Beatles, Queen, King's X, the Galactic Cowboys and Boston, my ears were suddenly attracted to an enormous cornucopia of musical versatility.

Through further studies, I then found myself exposed to 3 newer terms that I began wrapping my ever-curious young, expanding mind around: **Polyrhythms**, **Polymeters** and **Ostinatos**. What were these? What did they mean? And how were they going to affect my playing and my evolution on my instrument? Piece by piece, I assembled my arsenal of weapons as each day became an educational leap into new territory. The first exposure to the soloistic creative ostinato by Max Roach in "The Drum Also Waltzes" lead me to the brilliant instructional video entitled "Solo Drums" by Terry Bozzio, soon to be followed up by the multi-pedal, rudimental footwork of Australian phenoms, Grant Collins and Chris Brien and eventually the dazzling left-foot clave work of former teacher and friend, Horacio "El Negro" Hernandez. Immediately I was hooked to the concept of the ostinato and "what the single drummer is able to do" with independent limb work.

Then, in 1992 at 19 years old, I had the honor and pleasure of studying with the late-great Pete Zeldman at The Drummers Collective in New York City (which would eventually become my home for teaching for the past 20 years of my life now). Pete exposed me to techniques, exercises, terms and applications of rhythms that I never thought were attainable by any drummer. That's the moment which solidified the aforementioned concept centered around "what is possible for a single drummer to achieve in any situation" (solo-wise, style-wise, etc.).

As a result of Pete's guidance, through the years, I developed my own systems of poly-oriented playing and instruction. However, I've noticed that generally students and players have had difficulties distinguishing between the term **"polymeter"** and **"polyrhythm"** – often times using the wrong term for what they are trying to describe in the music. In addition, there always is the ever-recurring question of, "Yeah, well, where can you use all of that stuff?" Understood. I see how it could be puzzling for those who have not experienced the utilization of this type of material. Fortunately, I grew up playing piano and composition is something I've done my whole life which has enabled me to apply these concepts in a musical fashion. I sympathize with those musicians who may not have the knowledge or background of another instrument.

For the past 30+ years of teaching this material, I have wanted to create a manual where all of my concepts can be found in one place. However, as I sat down and started constructing what lies before you, I discovered that there's far too much material to include in one single catalogue. I realized that I not only had to centralize my topic of choice but that I may have to split my concepts into separate volumes over time. So what you, the reader, are seeing is **Volume 1**, strictly in 4/4, of my concepts with conceivably more to come in the near future (including odd meter polymetric examples, 3rd layer ideas and multiple styles incorporating this abundance of material).

INTRODUCTION

POLYRHTHM vs. POLYMETER

As you enter the material in this book, I think the most important characteristic to bring up is the difference between a **"polyrhythm"** and a **"polymeter."** As mentioned earlier, these terms are often used interchangeably or mistaken for one another. I find that the majority of the Rock music we listen to such as Tool (with Danny Carey), Porcupine Tree (with Gavin Harrison), Meshuggah (with Tomas Haake) or even solo material by drummers such as Virgil Donati comprises of cyclical rhythmic phrases that fit into a **POLYMETRIC** category and yet often mistakenly referred to as being polyrhythmic. However, a composition like Frank Zappa's "The Black Page" or even some Jazz drummers such as Ari Hoenig, Bill Stewart or Dan Weiss (often using Eastern rhythms in their playing) are displaying more **polyrhythmic** playing.

When describing a polymeter, I describe these ideas as cyclical phrases that carry over the bar line (often referred to as "cross rhythms " or even "over the bar rhythms"), based on placement of accents or note groupings or rests in your pattern(s). These rhythmic cycles often reset after a number of set measures, depending on what groupings are falling over each other (4 over 3, 5 over 7, etc...). This transcribed example contains rests on every third 8th note of four 8th note groupings and it takes 3 full measures to reset itself, displaying an example of a **3 OVER 4 polymeter**:

However, when identifying a polyrhythm, I describe these ideas as specific note groups which fall against each other in the same window of time. Typically, these groups reset at the beginning of each measure or each "beat 1" of the group itself. Polyrhythms are less considered rhythmic "cycles" yet have more tension due to the friction of notes falling against one another in their given subdivision of time. Here would be an example of a **3 AGAINST 4 polyrhythm**:

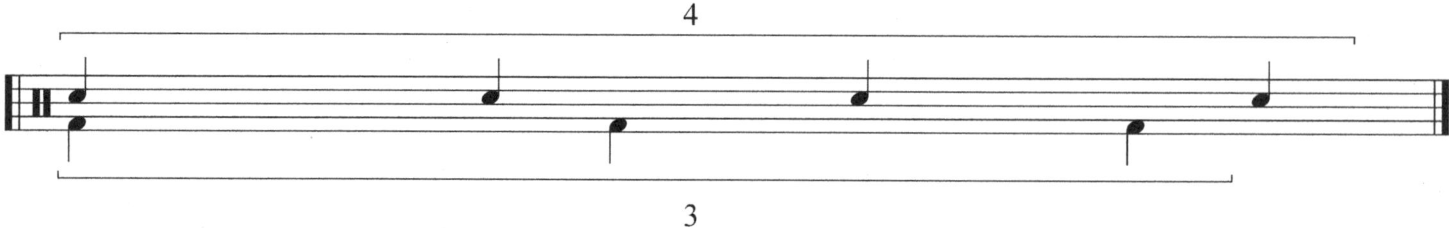

As a result of polymeters being more cyclical in nature and containing less rhythmic friction, it makes more sense that polymeters are applied to more of the music we listen to and play. Hence, what you're hearing, reading and playing in this book is a polymetric-based book and not typically considered polyrhythmic-based.

INTRODUCTION

FINAL NOTES

It is obvious that both polymeters and polyrhythms are quite challenging and can be easily frowned upon by other musicians that you may work with in a live, rehearsal or recording setting. However, if used at the correct times and/or in the correct manner, these musical characteristics can greatly influence your drum patterns/parts which, in turn, will enhance the song/performance itself.

Many people ask questions such as "When is the right time that I can use these in a musical setting" or "When will I ever use this material?" Planning out the correct timing in the most appropriate setting is definitely the key to the use of polymeters or polyrhythms. Here are some suggestions of knowing when the correct time to create or apply these to your own patterns:

A) Listen for odd-looped patterns from the guitar, horns, keyboard/piano or even the vocals. That way, it will give you a launching pad or an invitation to duplicate that cyclical rhythm on one (or more) of your limbs. Don't be afraid to ask "What is that pattern you're playing" or "how many notes are in that odd pattern?" If you can find that out from another musician and are able to then import that information into a drum groove, you can create great, innovative parts. Other musicians & their phrases are often times very helpful to what you generate behind the drum set.

B) Be aware of moments where the drums are featured (e.g. in a solo section) or where the song may depend on the drum pattern as being part of the "hook" of the song. This may give you an open door to create a poly-oriented groove.

C) Make sure to continually improve your reading and transcription skills. This will allow you to obtain the ability to create endless patterns as polymeters may often depend on transcribing ideas first.

D) If you are in a fusion, progressive or metal band, they provide a lot more of obvious settings for creating these more difficult patterns. Although, if you're able to put less stress on your accents or orchestration in your difficult patterns without interfering with the other instrumentation, even basic polymeters can be used in less demanding circumstances.

E) Polymeters are a great aid in the approach to improving your independence control or even your own long-extended drum solo. Soloing over ostinatos, applying poly-oriented playing to various styles, learning how to place various groupings and time variations against each other (etc...) can only augment your understanding of time and musicality. In addition, by studying how to make polymeters groove or work together, it will only improve the awareness of your internal clock overall.

And most of all, have fun learning any new material you are first experiencing! Good luck!!

FOREWORD

by David Garibaldi

When Jason approached me about writing something for his book, I wasn't sure if I was the right person for the job. But, as I look through the pages, I see the work of someone who has vision for himself and someone who has pushed himself to the heights of his vision. I can relate to this. Our collective goal should always be to creatively enhance the musical situations we find ourselves in. One of the very first things I ask people that I work with is what do you want to achieve? Do you have vision for yourself? Reading the introduction about what inspired him on his journey inspires me. Vision is a path, and if you follow it, you'll achieve things way beyond what you can imagine. This book is an example of what happens when you follow the path that's in front of you. Create with what you learn. We study so that we can create and add flavor to the musical situations we find ourselves in. This work will give you some new tools to build your groove by challenging your coordination in some very cool and new ways. Every chapter here builds on the previous one thoughtfully and logically, so if you go slow and stay consistent in your practice, great results will come. Have fun and **ENJOY**...!!!

Jason with David at the Aruba Jazz Festival in 1993. David on tour with Patti Austin, Jason on a family vacation!

David Garibaldi

David Garibaldi

PART 1

Cross-Rhythmic Grooves with 8th Note Rates

Section 1: Groupings of 3 (3/8 over 4/4)

In a normal 4/4 meter comprising of consistent 8th notes on the HH, it's safe to assume that one would eventually incorporate accents on downbeats to enhance the feel, sound and presence of the groove. The majority of drummers & instructors utilize and/or teach the usage of the Moeller technique to accurately execute the correct application of the accents. The breakdown of that HH pattern alone would look like this:

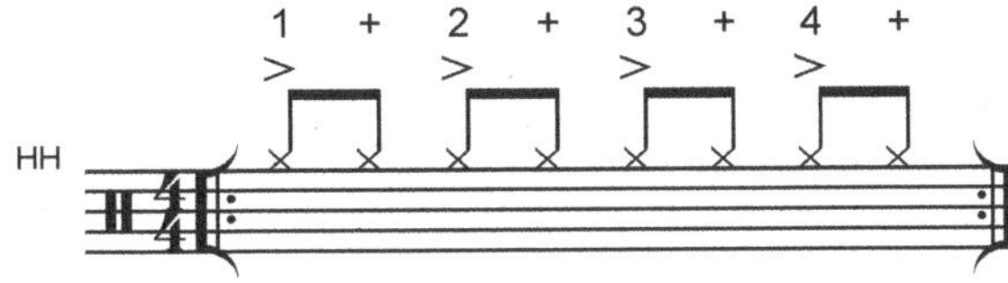

Adding the BD and SD in their proper places to create a "standard groove," the complete pattern is the very recognizable one seen here:

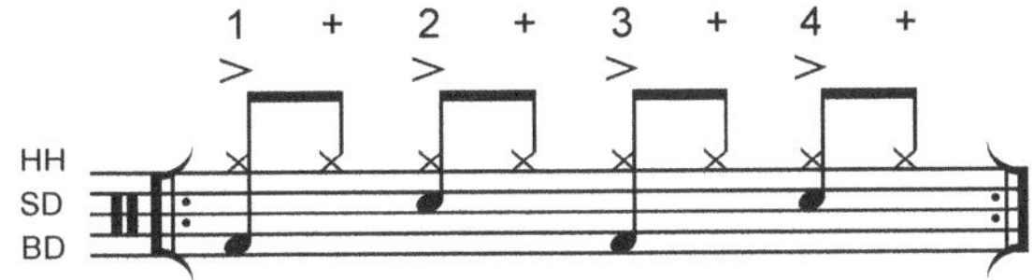

Notice that the above "standard groove" doesn't incorporate any cross rhythmic activity due to the accents laying in groupings of "2" and being in sync with the BD & SD pattern. However, in order to start displacing the accents and creating cross rhythmic ideas in a groove setting, a good place to start is to incorporate other numbered groupings in the time hand or limbs. Below is the breakdown of the same HH pattern but now utilizing groupings of "3" to create an "over the bar" rhythm. Take note that it takes 3 full measures to come back around to the downbeat of 1 again.

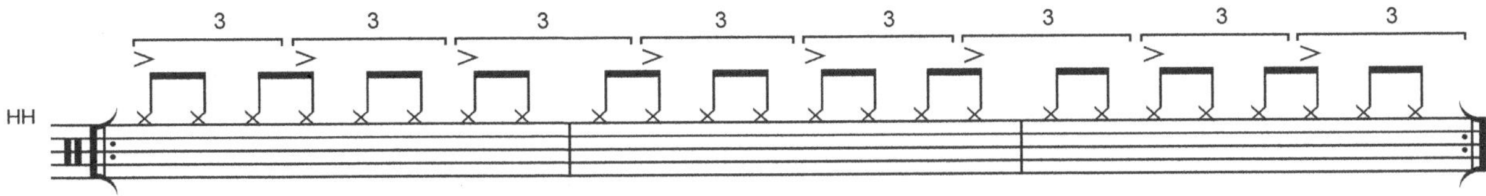

Tip: Counting Exercise

A good suggested exercise for any cross rhythm is to count out loud even before playing as to help build the two existing rhythms internally. Below, you will find a standard 3 measure phrase consisting of only 8th note counts, but every 3rd symbol is in **bold** as to represent the placement of an accent. Start by counting out loud, accentuating the bolded symbols while tapping your foot on downbeats in 4/4:

| **1** + 2 **+** 3 + **4** + | 1 **+** 2 + **3** + 4 **+** | 1 + **2** + 3 **+** 4 + |

Section 1

Groupings of 3 (3/8 over 4/4)

Primary Ostinato

The following pattern you see is the primary hand ostinato which will remain constant through the various grooves & exercises in this section. As your starting point, practice just this hand pattern together to develop independence involved in keeping the accents in groupings of "3" consistent over the top of the snare drum which remains on 2 & 4 throughout.

Practice Note: To obtain the most successful sound & feel of this ostinato, make sure that you are incorporating a repetitive 3-stroke Moeller accent technique in your time hand while you retain a consistent backbeat technique in the snare hand. Make an effort to ensure that the shifting accents do not affect or change the motion in either hand.

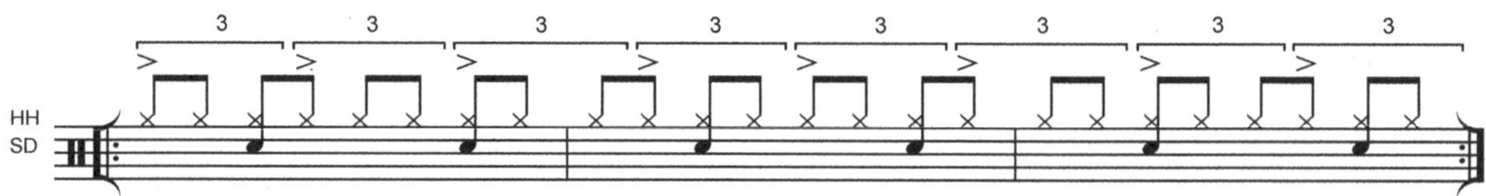

Incorporating the Bass Drum

The final goal is to now complete your phrases & grooves by adding countless bass drum rhythms to the ostinato. A great place to begin is to utilize any beginner drum set book with easy single-measure grooves. Since the full ostinato pattern with the groupings of "3" over the top is 3 measures long, you will need to play the single-measure grooves for 3 measures. Then, add an accent every 3 notes over the top of your HH pattern for everything to line up properly. Here is a starting point, using a "standard groove:"

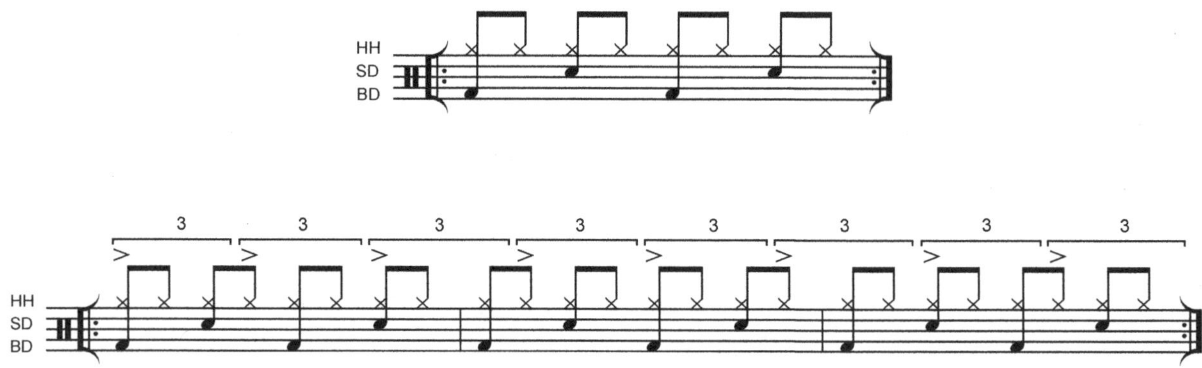

Exercise 1: Basic Beats

8th note rate grooves with groupings of 3 (3/8)

Below, you will find the transcription of the current ostinato once again. The rest of the page contains variations of simple grooves for bass drum variations. There are 3 ways you can go about working on these exercise pages for independence & variation development:

1) On a separate piece of paper, write out the ostinato 12 times. Extract the bass drum notes from the 12 single-measure grooves below and insert them into the ostinato phrases you've transcribed.

2) Play the single-measure phrases 3 times each and insert the accents (by ear) over the top of the grooves you are playing.

3) If you have a physical copy of the book, simply pencil in a bass drum pattern from a single-measure phrase into the ostinato. Once comfortable, erase and then move to transcribing the next patterns down the page one-by-one.

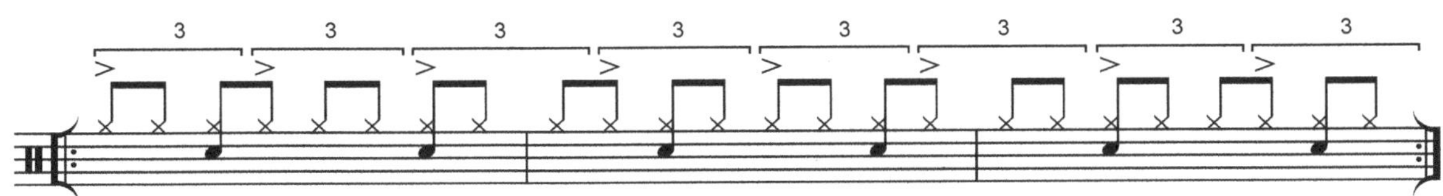

1 

2 

3 

4 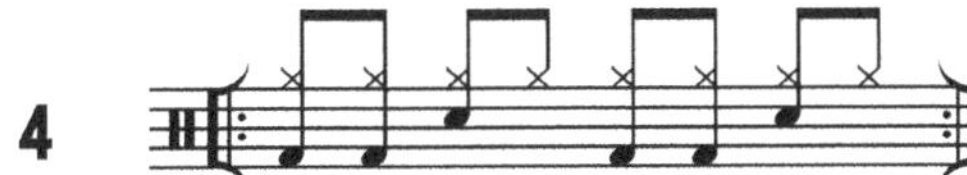

5 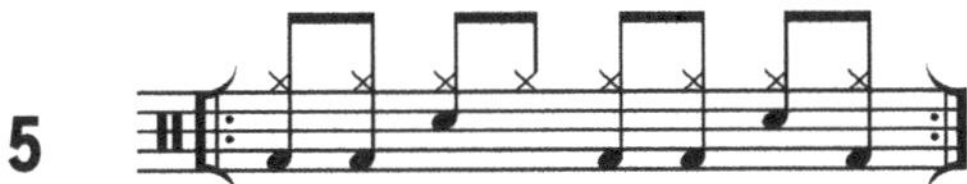

6 

7 

8 

9 

10 

11 

12 

Incorporating a Syncopated Bass Drum Moving Melody

Part 1: Quarter Notes and 8th Notes

The next step in varying your bass drum would be to combine an individual syncopated ongoing melody with the current ostinato. The melody you will see in the next section is written as if it were a snare melody, but you have the option of applying it to any limb that is applied to the kit. For the current exercises, we will be applying it to or playing it on the bass drum. The most appropriate book to use in this current rhythmic category is *Syncopation for the Modern Drummer* by Ted Reed. The full melody is an example of a page you will find in that book.

Below, find the example of line 1 of the syncopated exercise (found on the next page) and how it is then applied to the bass drum under the current ostinato with groupings of "3." Notice how you're only seeing the first 3 measures of the full melody exercise. Keep in mind that, as in the past few pages, ostinatos containing groupings of "3" will only create 3 bar phrases total in order to come back to your starting point again. Here is an illustration of the combination process, putting the hand pattern and the bass drum melody together.

Primary Ostinato

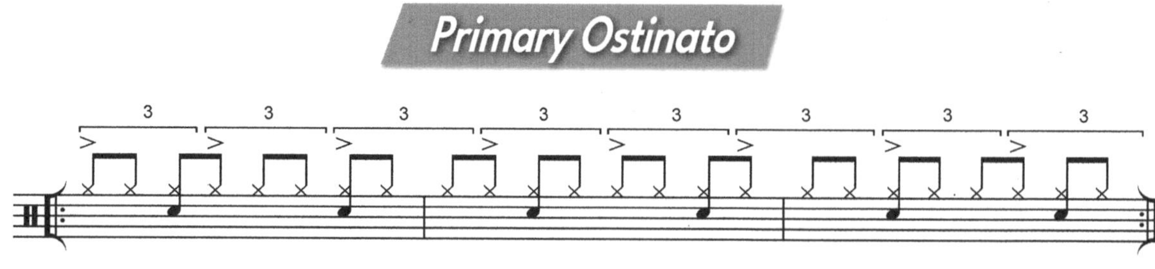

Bass Drum Melody (first 3 measures)

Combination (full phrase)

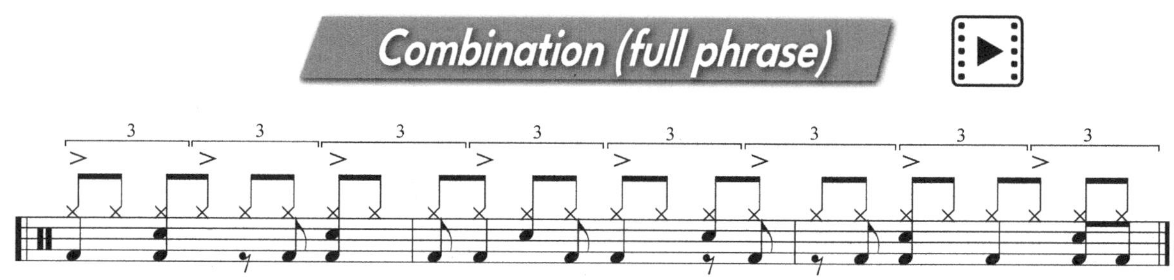

Exercise 2 : Syncopated Moving Melody with Quarters and 8ths

8th note rate grooves with groupings of 3 (3/8)

Below, you will find the transcription of the current ostinato once again. The rest of the page contains the entire rhythmic melody that will be applied to the bass drum. There are 3 ways you can go about working on these exercise pages for independence & variation development:

1) On a separate piece of paper, write out the ostinato 8 times. Insert the bass drum notes from the melody below into the ostinato phrases you've transcribed.

2) Play down the whole exercise/melody and insert the accents (by ear) over the top of the exercise you are playing.

3) If you have a physical copy of the book, simply pencil in 8th notes over the top of the melody and then write in an accent over every 3rd 8th note.

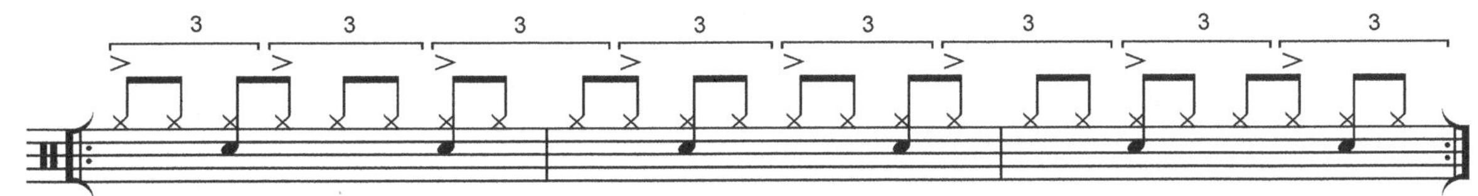

**Asterisks designate the measures where the accented groupings & phrases of "3" will reset on beat 1 again*

Incorporating a Syncopated Bass Drum Moving Melody

Part 2: Quarter Notes, 8th Notes and 16th Notes

Furthering your independence in varying your bass drum, the next step would be to incorporate variations of 16th notes within the ongoing melody and then combing that with the current ostinato. The melody you will see in the next section is written as if it were a snare melody, but you have the option of applying it to any limb that is applied to the kit. As with the previous exercises, we will be applying it to or playing it on the bass drum. The most appropriate book to use in this current rhythmic category is *The New Breed* by Gary Chester. The full melody in this section is an example of a page you will find in that book.

Below, find the example of line 1 of the exercise (found on the next page) and how it is then applied to the bass drum under the current ostinato with groupings of "3." Notice how you're only seeing the first 3 measures of the full melody exercise. Keep in mind that, as in the past few pages, ostinatos containing groupings of "3" will only create 3 bar phrases total in order to come back to your starting point again. Here is an illustration of the combination process, putting the hand pattern and the bass drum melody together.

Primary Ostinato

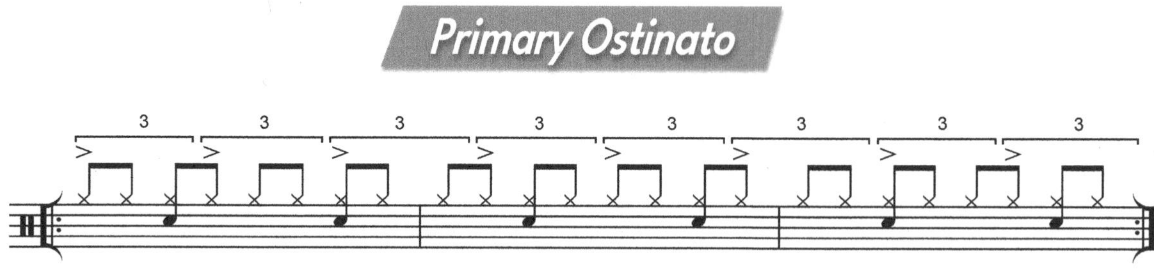

Bass Drum Melody (first 3 measures)

Combination (full phrase)

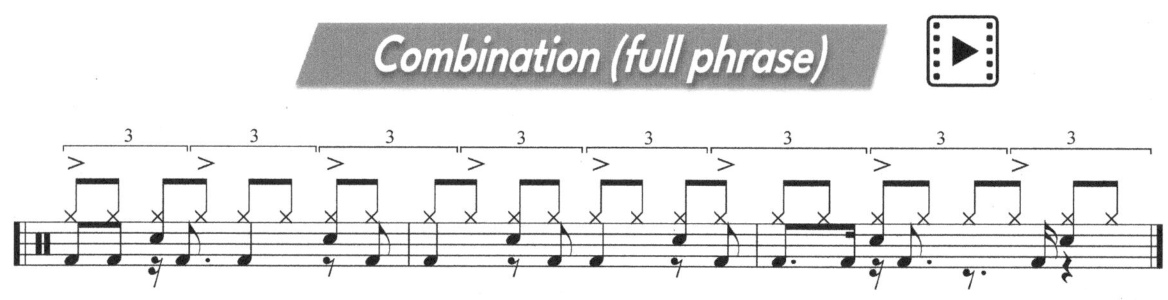

Exercise 3: Syncopated Moving Melody with Quarter Notes, 8th Notes and 16th Notes

8th note rate grooves with groupings of 3 (3/8)

Below, you will find the transcription of the current ostinato once again. The rest of the page contains the entire rhythmic melody that will be applied to the bass drum. There are 3 ways you can go about working on these exercise pages for independence & variation development:

1) On a separate piece of paper, write out the ostinato 8 times. Insert the bass drum notes from the melody below into the ostinato phrases you've transcribed.

2) Play down the whole exercise/melody and insert the accents (by ear) over the top of the exercise you are playing.

3) If you have a physical copy of the book, simply pencil in 8th notes over the top of the melody and then write in an accent over every 3rd 8th note.

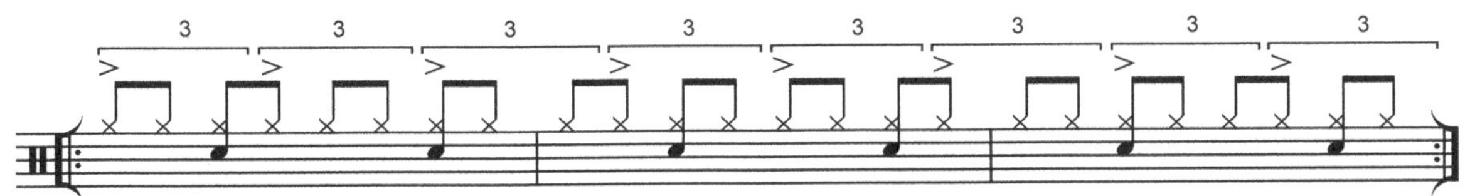

**Asterisks designate the measures where the accented groupings & phrases of "3" will reset on beat 1 again*

Section 2: Groupings of 5 (5/8 over 4/4)

After you feel comfortable working with groupings of "3" in your time hand, a sensible step is to move toward groupings of "5." Below is the breakdown of the HH pattern but now utilizing groupings of "5" to create a larger "over the bar" rhythm. Keep in mind that it now takes 5 full measures to come back around to the downbeat of 1 again.

***Note*:** There are several ways to play or perform the accents in groupings of "5." Playing one accent every 5 notes is a standard approach. However, it's often more musical and/or pleasing to the ear to subdivide the groupings such as a 2+3 or 3+2 phrasing. For practicality & musical purposes, the phrases you see will be organized with a 2+3 phrasing.

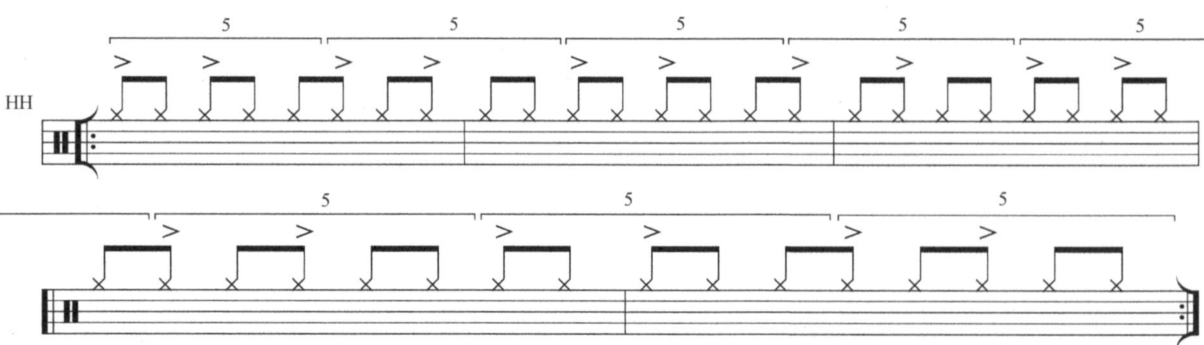

Tip: Counting Exercise

Remember that a good suggested exercise for any cross rhythm is to count out loud even before playing as to help build the two existing rhythms internally. Below, you will find a standard 5 measure phrase consisting of only 8th note counts, but every **bolded** number or symbol represents the placement of an accent. This time, the bolded counts reflect the 2+3 subdivided phrase listed above. Start by counting out loud, accentuating the bolded symbols while tapping your foot on downbeats in 4/4:

| **1** + **2** + 3 **+** 4 **+** | 1 + **2** + **3** + 4 **+** | 1 **+** 2 + **3** + **4** + |

| 1 **+** 2 **+** 3 + **4** + | **1** + 2 **+** 3 **+** 4 + |

Section 2
Groupings of 5 (5/8 over 4/4)

The following pattern you see is the primary hand ostinato which will remain constant through the various grooves & exercises in this section. As your starting point, practice just this hand pattern together to develop independence involved in keeping the accents, this time, in groupings of "5," consistent over the top of the snare drum which remains on beats 2 & 4 throughout. Remember that the subdivision break up for your groupings of "5" is a 2+3 phrase.

Practice Note: To obtain the most successful sound & feel of this ostinato, make sure that you are incorporating a repetitive Moeller accent technique in 2 strokes, then 3 strokes, each phrase in your time hand while you retain a consistent backbeat technique in the snare hand. Make an effort to ensure that the shifting accents do not affect or change the motion in either hand.

Primary Ostinato

Incorporating the Bass Drum

Similar to the previous section in this chapter, the final goal is to now complete your phrases & grooves by adding countless bass drum rhythms to the ostinato. A great place to begin is to utilize any beginner drum set book with easy single-measure grooves. Since the full ostinato pattern with the groupings of "5" over the top is 5 measures long, you will need to play the single-measure grooves for 5 measures. Then, add the 2+3 phrases of "5" over the top of your HH pattern for everything to line up properly. Here is a starting point, using a "standard groove:"

HH
SD
BD

Exercise 4 : Basic Beats

8th note rate grooves with groupings of 5 (5/8)

Below, you will find the transcription of the current ostinato once again. The rest of the page contains the same previous variations of simple grooves for bass drum variations. There are 3 ways you can go about working on these exercise pages for independence & variation development:

1) On a separate piece of paper, write out the ostinato 12 times. Extract the bass drum notes from the 12 single-measure grooves below and insert them into the ostinato phrases you've transcribed.

2) Play the single-measure phrases 5 times each and insert the accents (by ear) over the top of the grooves you are playing.

3) If you have a physical copy of the book, simply pencil in a bass drum pattern from a single-measure phrase into the ostinato below. Once comfortable, erase and then move to transcribing the next patterns down the page one-by-one.

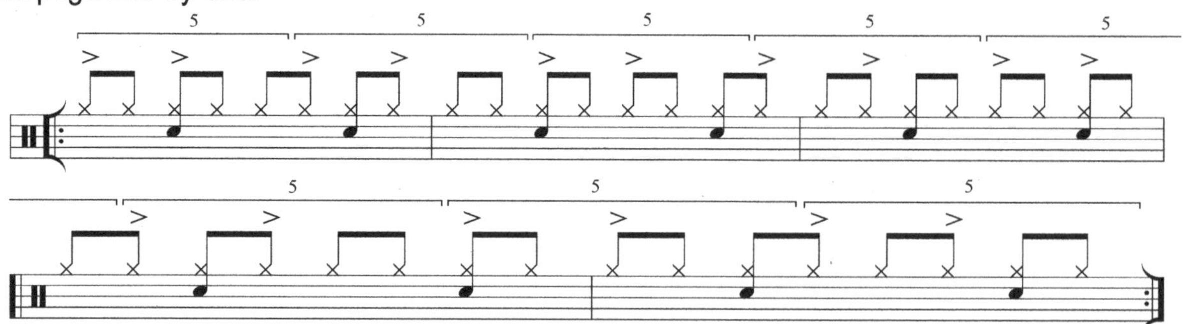

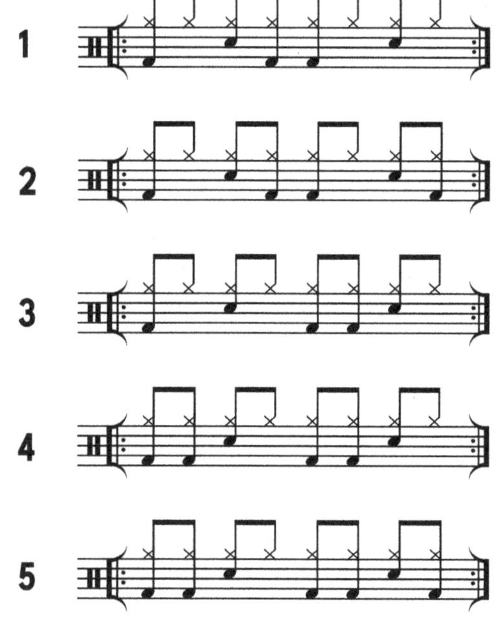

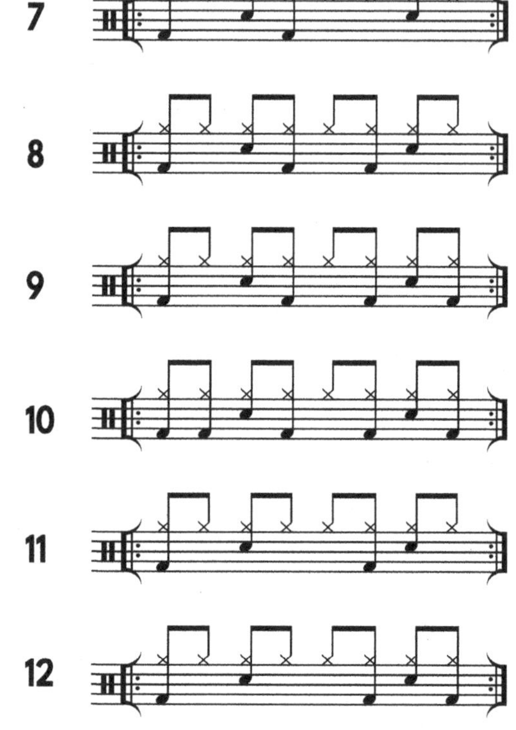

Incorporating a Syncopated Bass Drum Moving Melody

Part 1: Quarter Notes and 8th Notes

As in the previous section, the next step in varying your bass drum would be to combine an individual syncopated ongoing melody with the current ostinato. The melody you will see in the next section is written as if it were a snare melody, but you have the option of applying it to any limb that is applied to the kit. For the current exercises, we will still be applying it to or playing it on the bass drum. The most appropriate book to use in this current rhythmic category is *Syncopation for the Modern Drummer* by Ted Reed. The full melody is an example of a page you will find in that book.

Below, find the first 5 measures of the syncopated exercise (found on the next page) and how it is then applied to the bass drum under the current ostinato with groupings of "5." Notice how you're only seeing the first 5 measures of the full melody exercise. Keep in mind that, as in the past few pages, ostinatos containing groupings of "5" will create 5 bar phrases total in order to come back to your starting point again. Here is an illustration of the combination process, putting the hand pattern and the bass drum melody together.

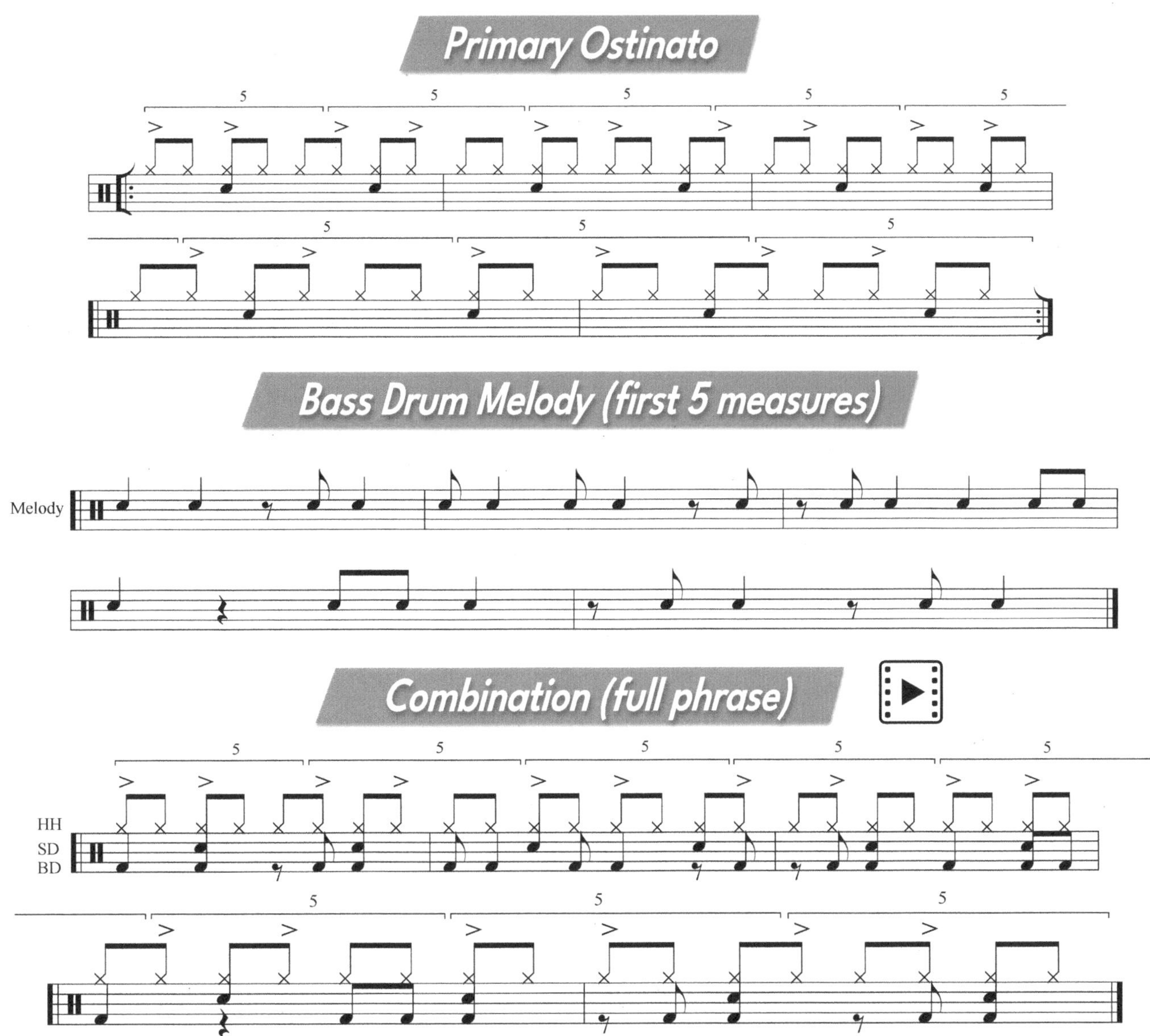

Exercise 5 : Syncopated Moving Melody with Quarters and 8ths

8th note rate grooves with groupings of 5 (5/8)

Below, you will find the transcription of the current ostinato once again. The rest of the page contains the entire rhythmic melody that will be applied to the bass drum. There are 3 ways you can go about working on these exercise pages for independence & variation development:

1) On a separate piece of paper, write out the ostinato several times. Insert the bass drum notes from the melody below into the ostinato phrases you've transcribed.

2) Play down the whole exercise/melody and insert the accents (by ear) over the top of the exercise you are playing.

3) If you have a physical copy of the book, simply pencil in 8th notes over the top of the melody and then write in 2+3 groupings over the ongoing 8th notes.

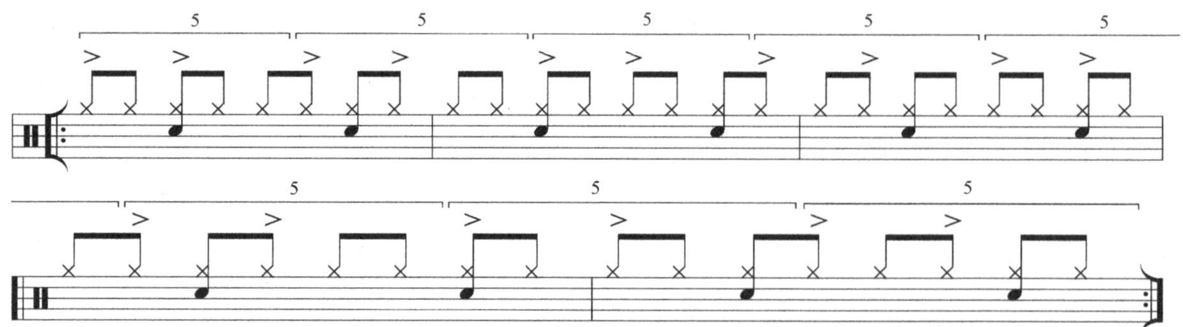

**Asterisks designate the measures where the accented groupings & phrases of "5" will reset on beat 1 again*

Incorporating a Syncopated Bass Drum Moving Melody

Part 2: Quarter Notes, 8th Notes and 16th Notes

Similar to the previous section of this chapter, the next step would be to incorporate variations of 16th notes within the ongoing melody and then combing that with the current ostinato. The melody you will see in the next section is written as if it were a snare melody, but you have the option of applying it to any limb that is applied to the kit. As with the previous exercises, we will be applying it to or playing it on the bass drum. The most appropriate book to use in this current rhythmic category is *The New Breed* by Gary Chester. The full melody in this section is an example of a page you will find in that book.

Below, find the first 5 measures of the exercise (found on the next page) and how it is then applied to the bass drum under the current ostinato with groupings of "5." Notice how you're only seeing the first 5 measures of the full melody exercise. Keep in mind that, as in the past few pages, ostinatos containing groupings of "5" will create 5 bar phrases total in order to come back to your starting point again. Here is an illustration of the combination process, putting the hand pattern and the bass drum melody together.

Primary Ostinato

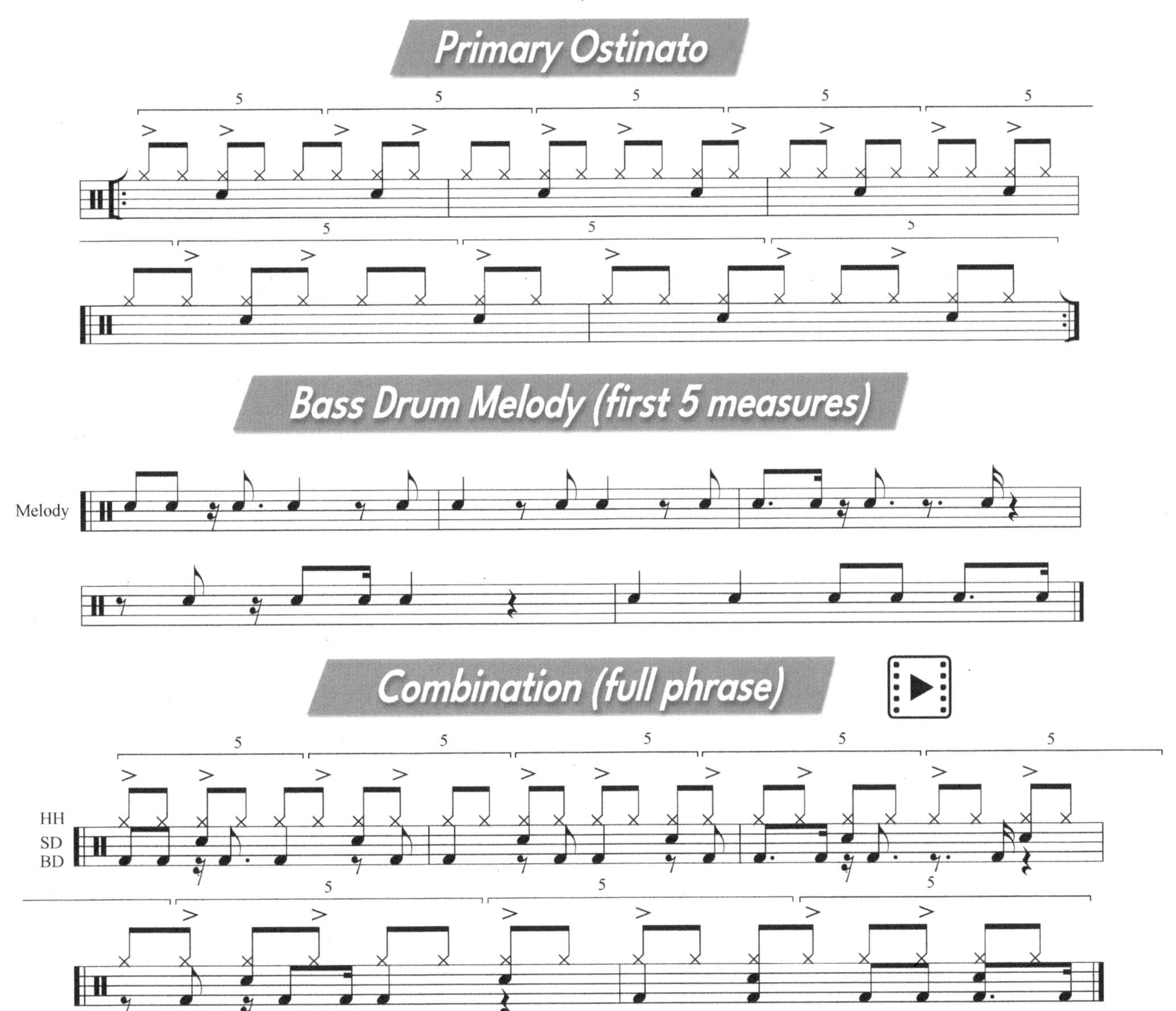

Exercise 6: Syncopated Moving Melody with Quarter Notes, 8th Notes and 16th Notes

8th note rate grooves with groupings of 5 (5/8)

Below, you will find the transcription of the current ostinato once again. The rest of the page contains the entire rhythmic melody that will be applied to the bass drum. There are 3 ways you can go about working on these exercise pages for independence & variation development:

1) On a separate piece of paper, write out the ostinato several times. Insert the bass drum notes from the melody below into the ostinato phrases you've transcribed.

2) Play down the whole exercise/melody and insert the accents (by ear) over the top of the exercise you are playing.

3) If you have a physical copy of the book, simply pencil in 8th notes over the top of the melody and then write in 2+3 groupings over the ongoing 8th notes.

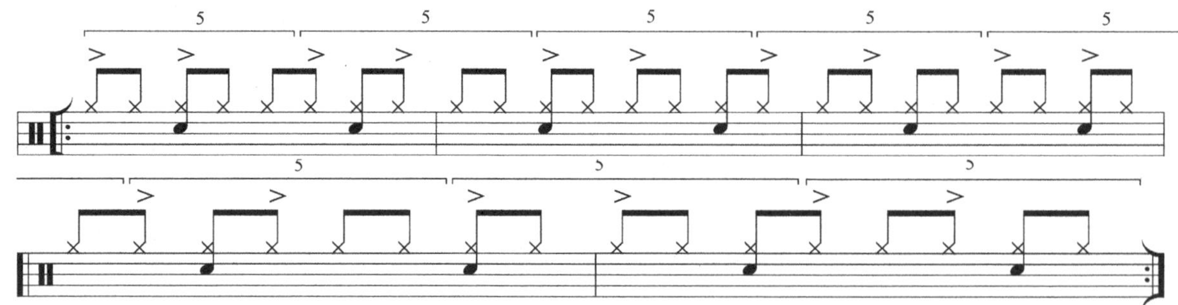

Asterisks designate the measures where the accented groupings & phrases of "5" will reset on beat 1 again

Section 3: Groupings of 7 (7/8 over 4/4)

After you feel comfortable working with groupings of "5" in your time hand, a sensible step is to move toward groupings of "7." Below is the breakdown of the HH pattern but now utilizing groupings of "7" to create an even larger "over the bar" rhythm. Keep in mind that it now takes 7 full measures to come back around to the downbeat of 1 again.

***Note*:** There are several ways to play or perform the accents in groupings of "7." Playing one accent every 7 notes is a standard approach. However, it's often more musical and/or pleasing to the ear to subdivide the groupings such as a 2+2+3 or 3+2+2 phrasing (even a 2+3+2 phrasing is used). For practicality & musical purposes, the phrases you see will be organized with a 2+2+3 phrasing.

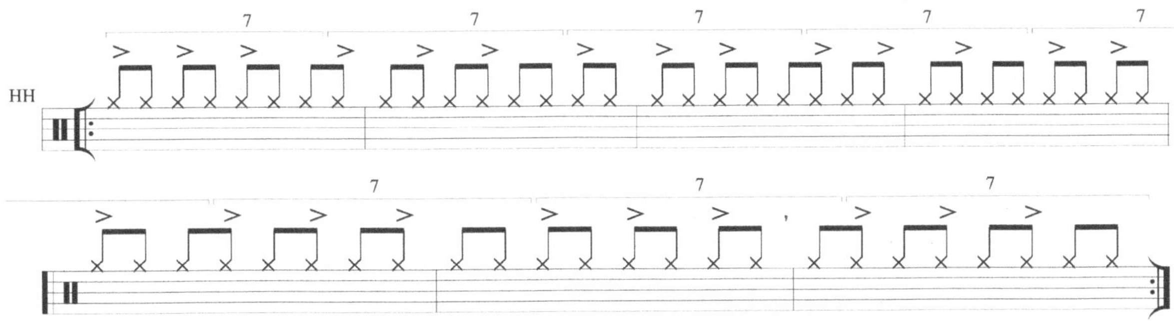

Tip: Counting Exercise

Remember that a good suggested exercise for any cross rhythm is to count out loud even before playing as to help build the two existing rhythms internally. Below, you will find a standard 7 measure phrase consisting of only 8th note counts, but every **bolded** number or symbol represents the placement of an accent. This time, the bolded counts reflect the 2+2+3 subdivided phrase listed above. Start by counting out loud, accentuating the bolded symbols while tapping your foot on downbeats in 4/4:

| **1** + **2** + **3** + 4 **+** | 1 **+** 2 **+** 3 + **4** + | **1** + **2** + 3 **+** 4 **+** | 1 **+** 2 + **3** + **4** + |

| **1** + 2 **+** 3 **+** 4 **+** | 1 + **2** + **3** + **4** + | 1 **+** 2 **+** 3 **+** 4 + |

The following pattern you see is the primary hand ostinato which will remain constant through the various grooves & exercises in this next section. As your starting point, practice just this hand pattern together to develop independence involved in keeping the accents, this time, in groupings of "7," consistent over the top of the snare drum which remains on beats 2 & 4 throughout. Remember that the subdivision break up for your groupings of "7" is a 2+2+3 phrase.

Practice Note: To obtain the most successful sound & feel of this ostinato, make sure that you are incorporating a repetitive Moeller accent technique in 2 strokes, 2 strokes again, then 3 strokes each phrase in your time hand while you retain a consistent backbeat technique in the snare hand. Make an effort to ensure that the shifting accents do not affect or change the motion in either hand.

Primary Ostinato

Incorporating the Bass Drum

Similar to the previous sections in this chapter, the final goal is to now complete your phrases & grooves by adding countless bass drum rhythms to the ostinato. A great place to begin is to utilize any beginner drum set book with easy single-measure grooves. Since the full ostinato pattern with the groupings of "7" over the top is 7 measures long, you will need to play the single-measure grooves for 7 measures. Then, add the 2+2+3 phrases of "7" over the top of your HH pattern for everything to line up properly. Here is a starting point, using a "standard groove:"

Exercise 7: Basic Beats

8th note rate grooves with groupings of 7 (7/8)

Below, you will find the transcription of the current ostinato once again. The rest of the page contains the same previous variations of simple grooves for bass drum variations. There are 3 ways you can go about working on these exercise pages for independence & variation development:

1) On a separate piece of paper, write out the ostinato 12 times. Extract the bass drum notes from the 12 single-measure grooves below and insert them into the ostinato phrases you've transcribed.

2) Play the single-measure phrases 7 times each and insert the accents (by ear) over the top of the grooves you are playing.

3) If you have a physical copy of the book, simply pencil in a bass drum pattern from a single-measure phrase into the ostinato below. Once comfortable, erase and then move to transcribing the next patterns down the page one-by-one.

1 

2 

3 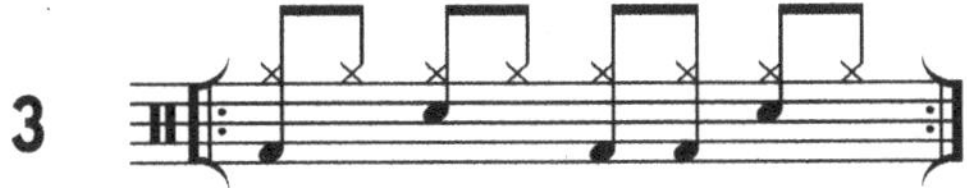

4 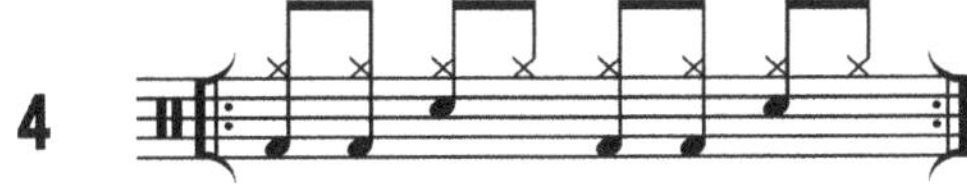

5 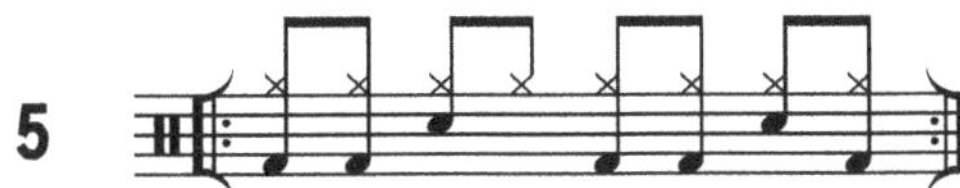

6 

7 

8 

9 

10 

11 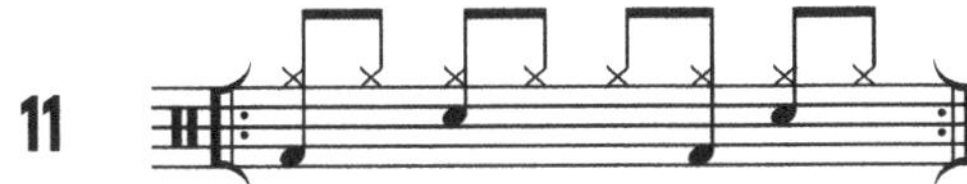

12 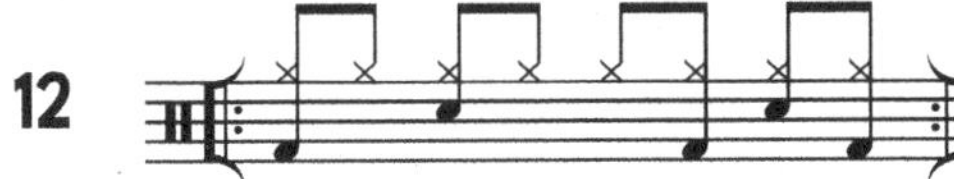

Incorporating a Syncopated Bass Drum Moving Melody

Part 1: Quarter Notes and 8th Notes

As in the previous section, the next step in varying your bass drum would be to combine an individual syncopated ongoing melody with the current ostinato. The melody you will see in the next section is written as if it were a snare melody, but you have the option of applying it to any limb that is applied to the kit. For the current exercises, we will still be applying it to or playing it on the bass drum. The most appropriate book to use in this current rhythmic category is *Syncopation for the Modern Drummer* by Ted Reed. The full melody is an example of a page you will find in that book.

Below, find the first 7 measures of the syncopated exercise (found on the next page) and how it is then applied to the bass drum under the current ostinato with groupings of "7." Notice how you're only seeing the first 7 measures of the full melody exercise. Keep in mind that, as in the past few pages, ostinatos containing groupings of "7" will create 7 bar phrases total in order to come back to your starting point again. Here is an illustration of the combination process, putting the hand pattern and the bass drum melody together.

Primary Ostinato

HH
SD

Bass Drum Melody (first 7 measures)

Melody

Combination (full phrase)

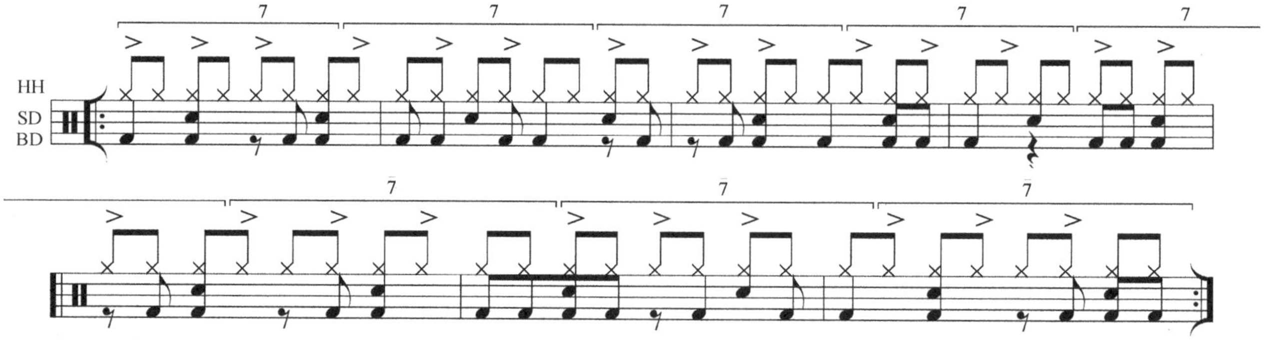

HH
SD
BD

Exercise 8 : Syncopated Moving Melody with Quarters and 8ths

8th note rate grooves with groupings of 7 (7/8)

Below, you will find the transcription of the current ostinato once again. The rest of the page contains the entire rhythmic melody that will be applied to the bass drum. There are 3 ways you can go about working on these exercise pages for independence & variation development:

1) On a separate piece of paper, write out the ostinato several times. Insert the bass drum notes from the melody below into the ostinato phrases you've transcribed.

2) Play down the whole exercise/melody and insert the accents (by ear) over the top of the exercise you are playing.

3) If you have a physical copy of the book, simply pencil in 8th notes over the top of the melody and then write in 2+2+3 groupings over the ongoing 8th notes.

**Asterisks designate the measures where the accented groupings & phrases of "7" will reset on beat 1 again*

Incorporating a Syncopated Bass Drum Moving Melody

Part 2: Quarter Notes, 8th Notes and 16th Notes

Similar to the previous section of this chapter, the next step would be to incorporate variations of 16th notes within the ongoing melody and then combing that with the current ostinato. The melody you will see in the next section is written as if it were a snare melody, but you have the option of applying it to any limb that is applied to the kit. As with the previous exercises, we will be applying it to or playing it on the bass drum. The most appropriate book to use in this current rhythmic category is *The New Breed* by Gary Chester. The full melody in this section is an example of a page you will find in that book.

Below, find the first 7 measures of the exercise (found on the next page) and how it is then applied to the bass drum under the current ostinato with groupings of "7." Notice how you're only seeing the first 7 measures of the full melody exercise. Keep in mind that, as in the past few pages, ostinatos containing groupings of "7" will create 7 bar phrases total in order to come back to your starting point again. Here is an illustration of the combination process, putting the hand pattern and the bass drum melody together.

Primary Ostinato

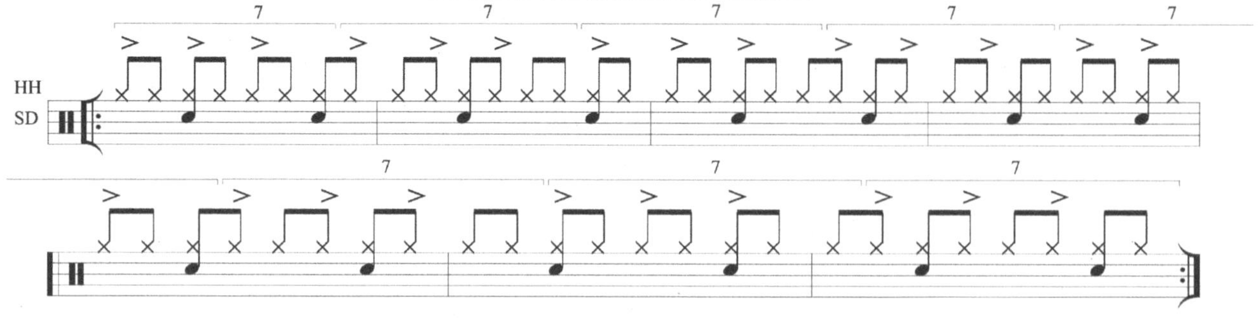

HH
SD

Bass Drum Melody (first 7 measures)

Melody

Combination (full phrase)

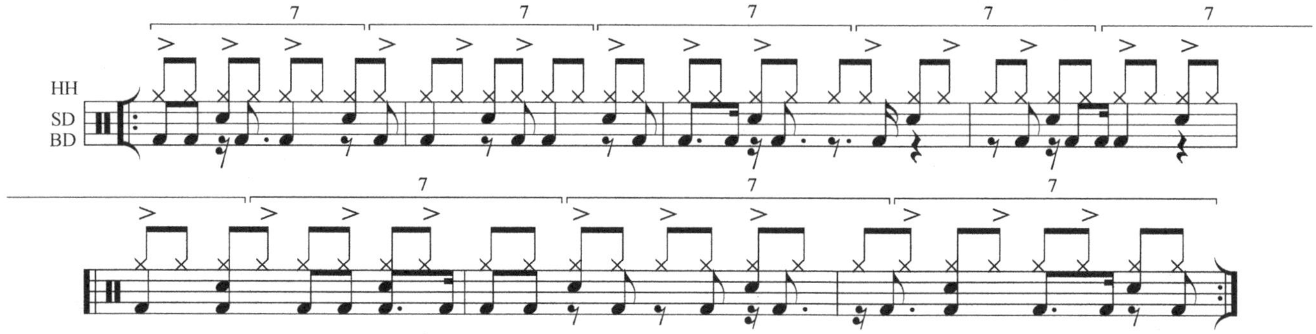

HH
SD
BD

Exercise 9: Syncopated Moving Melody with Quarter Notes, 8th Notes and 16th Notes

8th note rate grooves with groupings of 7 (7/8)

Below, you will find the transcription of the current ostinato once again. The rest of the page contains the entire rhythmic melody that will be applied to the bass drum. There are 3 ways you can go about working on these exercise pages for independence & variation development:

1) On a separate piece of paper, write out the ostinato several times. Insert the bass drum notes from the melody below into the ostinato phrases you've transcribed.

2) Play down the whole exercise/melody and insert the accents (by ear) over the top of the exercise you are playing.

3) If you have a physical copy of the book, simply pencil in 8th notes over the top of the melody and then write in 2+2+3 groupings over the ongoing 8th notes.

Asterisks designate the measures where the accented groupings & phrases of "7" will reset on beat 1 again

Section 4: Groove Displacement

Though the ostinatos have presented their own challenges with displacement or movement of "time," notice that the previous exercises throughout the chapter have been only inclusive of a standard groove or backbeat on 2 & 4 from the snare drum. To round out the material in this chapter, a challenging set of exercises centers around using the current ostinatos but now "assigning" the snare drum and bass drum to specific beats in order to cover the topic of ***displacement***.

Before attempting to jump into the polymetric combinations of rhythms, below is the explanation of a practical displacement method in a standard 4/4 meter with no cross rhythms.

***Note*:** The primary suggested exercises throughout this next section use only the current syncopated moving melody of quarter note, 8th note and 16th notes that has appeared on previous pages.

First 4 Measures of Melody

"Boxed-Off" Melody

In order to start assigning the bass drum & snare drum to proper beats, a good first step is to "box off" the melody so you can clearly see where beats 1, 2, 3 & 4 are located.

Development of Full Displaced Groove

Finally, play the bass drum & snare drum in their proper places by sticking with standard groove rules: Anything falling inside the boxes of 1 & 3 will be played on the bass drum; anything falling inside the boxes of 2 & 4 will be played on the snare drum. Shown below is the completed groove with the addition of standard HH 8th notes along with the bass drum & snare drum on their respective staff lines.

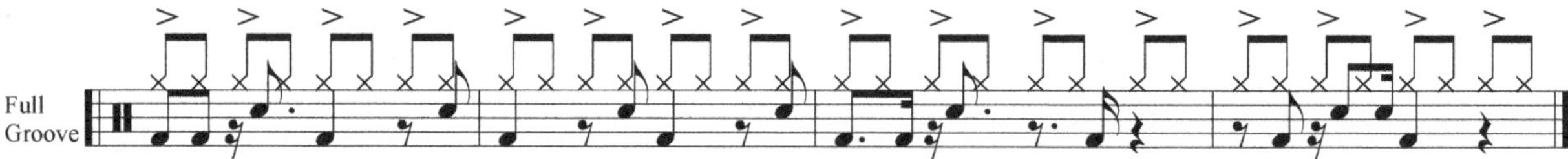

Incorporating the Ostinatos With the Displacement Method

Once you are comfortable with the process of assigning & displacing the melody onto the proper surfaces, the next step would be to apply the polymetric ostinatos to the exercises. Below, you will find a brief example each of the previous ostinatos combined with the process of displacement.

First 3 Measures of Melody

Ostinato With Groupings of 3 (or 3/8)

First 5 Measures of Melody

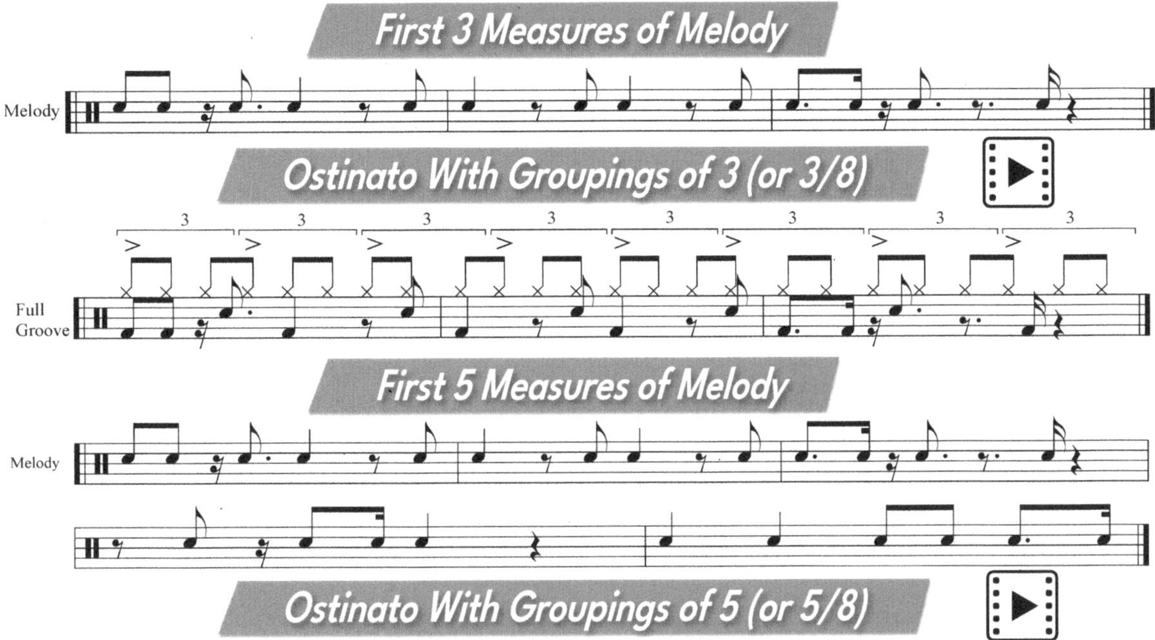

Ostinato With Groupings of 5 (or 5/8)

Here is the example of the melody displacement method combined with the ostinato with groupings of "5."
NOTE: You're only seeing the first 5 measures of the melody due to the phrase resetting after 5 measures.

First 7 Measures of Melody

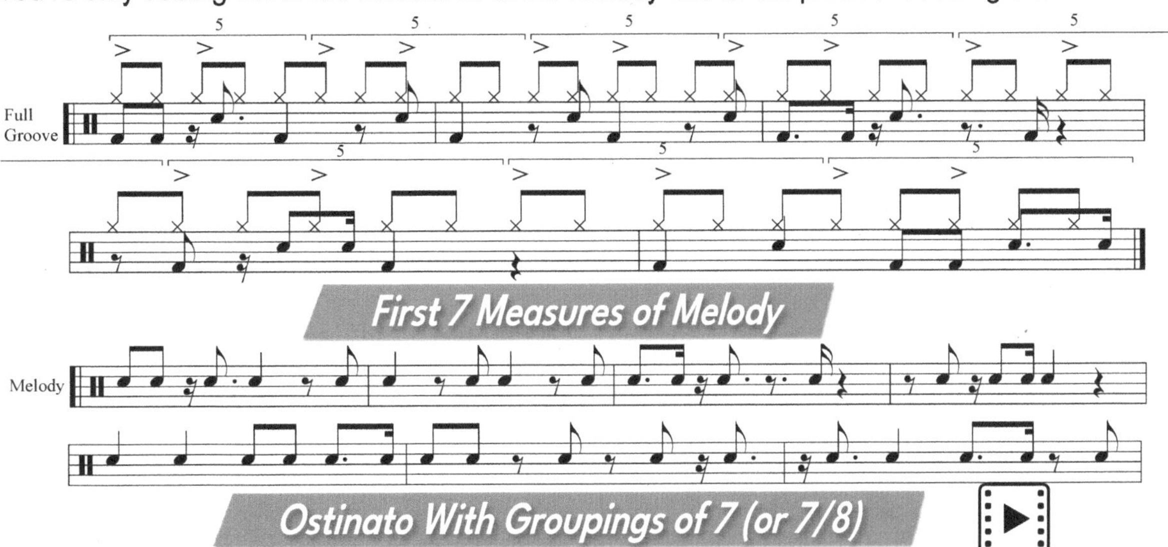

Ostinato With Groupings of 7 (or 7/8)

Here is the example of the melody displacement method combined with the ostinato with groupings of "7."
NOTE: You're only seeing the first 7 measures of the melody due to the phrase resetting after 7 measures.

Exercise 10: Incorporating Displaced Moving Melody With the Ostinato

8th note rate grooves with groupings of 3 (3/8)

Below, you will find transcription of the ostinato containing groupings of "3." However, this time, only the HH is included. Since the assignment utilizes movement of both bass drum & snare drum, the only constant pattern are the accents in the HH hand. The rest of the page contains the entire rhythmic melody that will be altered by assigning the bass drum & snare drum on the proper counts. There are 3 ways you can go about working on these exercise pages for independence & variation development:

1) On a separate piece of paper, write out the ostinato 8 times. Insert the assigned bass drum & snare drum notes from the melody below into the ostinato phrases you've transcribed.

2) Play down the whole exercise/melody and insert the accents (by ear) over the top of the exercise you are playing.

3) If you have a physical copy of the book, simply pencil in 8th notes over the top of the melody and then write in an accent over every 3rd 8th note.

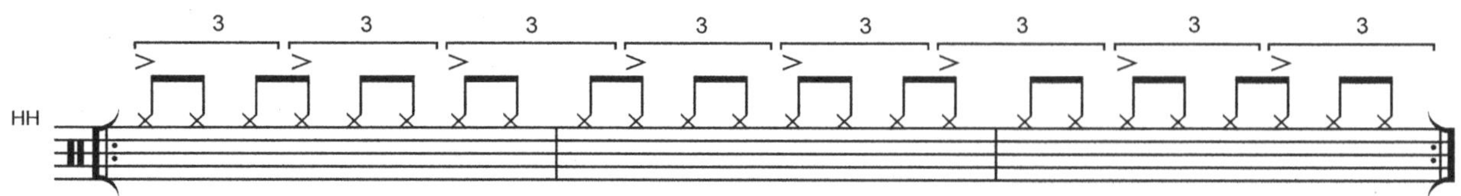

**Asterisks designate the measures where the accented groupings & phrases of "3" will reset on beat 1 again*

Exercise 11: Incorporating Displaced Moving Melody With the Ostinato

8th note rate grooves with groupings of 5 (5/8)

Below, you will find transcription of the ostinato containing groupings of "5." However, this time, only the HH is included. Since the assignment utilizes movement of both bass drum & snare drum, the only constant pattern are the accents in the HH hand. The rest of the page contains the entire rhythmic melody that will be altered by assigning the bass drum & snare drum on the proper counts. There are 3 ways you can go about working on these exercise pages for independence & variation development:

1) On a separate piece of paper, write out the ostinato several times. Insert the assigned bass drum & snare drum notes from the melody below into the ostinato phrases you've transcribed.

2) Play down the whole exercise/melody and insert the accents (by ear) over the top of the exercise you are playing.

3) If you have a physical copy of the book, simply pencil in 8th notes over the top of the melody and then write in an accent over every 3rd 8th note.

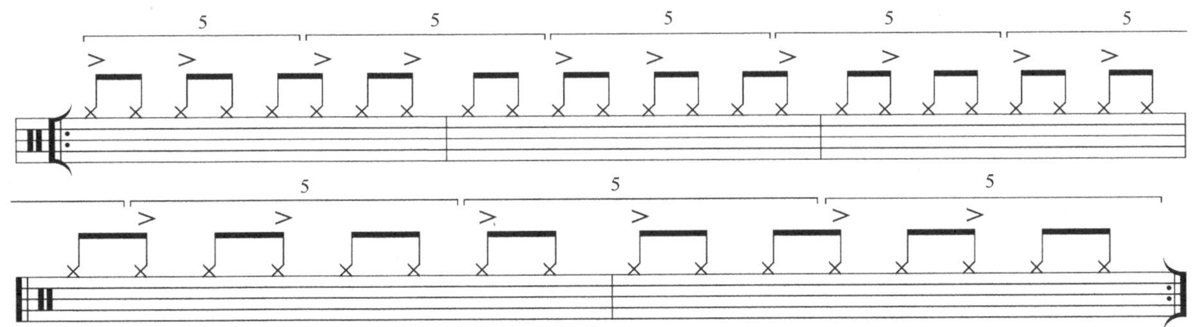

Asterisks designate the measures where the accented groupings & phrases of "5" will reset on beat 1 again

Exercise 12: Incorporating Displaced Moving Melody With the Ostinato

8th note rate grooves with groupings of 7 (7/8)

Below, you will find transcription of the ostinato containing groupings of "7." However, this time, only the HH is included. Since the assignment utilizes movement of both bass drum & snare drum, the only constant pattern are the accents in the HH hand. The rest of the page contains the entire rhythmic melody that will be altered by assigning the bass drum & snare drum on the proper counts. There are 3 ways you can go about working on these exercise pages for independence & variation development:

1) On a separate piece of paper, write out the ostinato several times. Insert the assigned bass drum & snare drum notes from the melody below into the ostinato phrases you've transcribed.

2) Play down the whole exercise/melody and insert the accents (by ear) over the top of the exercise you are playing.

3) If you have a physical copy of the book, simply pencil in 8th notes over the top of the melody and then write in an accent over every 2+2+3 8th notes.

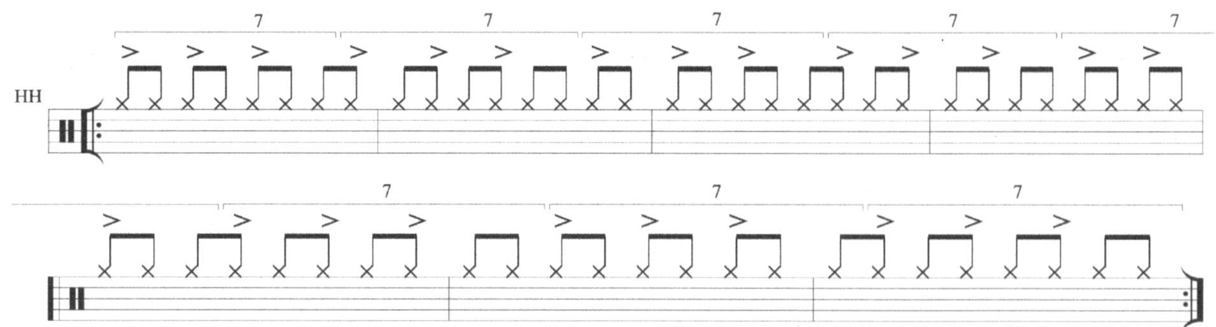

**Asterisks designate the measures where the accented groupings & phrases of "7" will reset on beat 1 again*

PART 2

CHANGE OF RATES

Cross-Rhythmic Grooves with 16th Note Rates

Section 1: Groupings of 3 (or 3/16) over 4/4

In a normal 4/4 meter comprising of consistent 16th notes on the HH, as with the 8th note rate in the previous chapter, it's safe to assume that one would eventually incorporate accents on downbeats to enhance the feel, sound and presence of the groove. The majority of drummers & instructors utilize and/or teach the usage of the Moeller technique to accurately execute the correct application of the accents. The breakdown of that HH pattern alone would look like this:

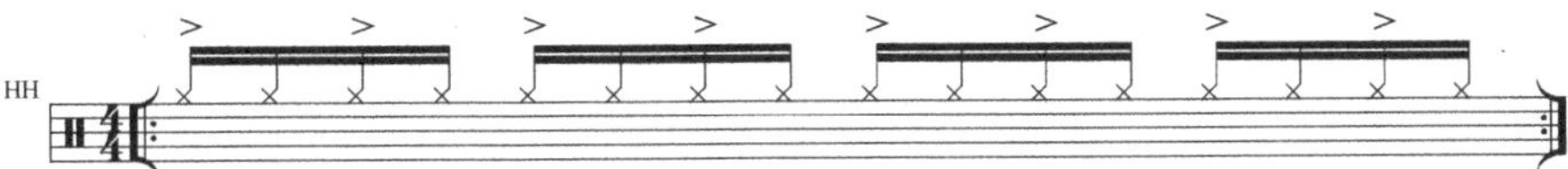

Adding the BD and SD in their proper places to create a "standard groove," the complete pattern is the very recognizable one seen here:

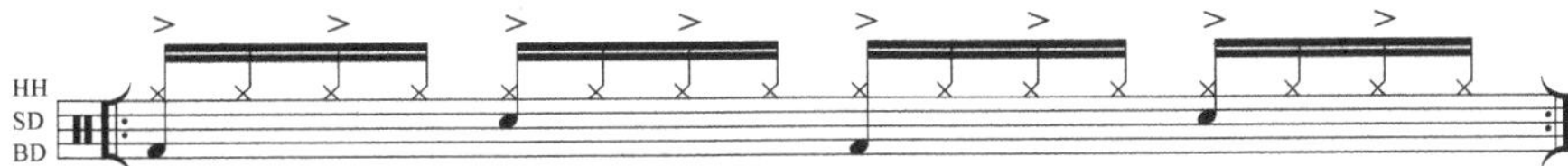

Notice that the above "standard groove" doesn't incorporate any cross rhythmic activity due to the accents laying in groupings of "2" and being in sync with the BD & SD pattern. However, in order to start displacing the accents and creating cross rhythmic ideas in a groove setting, a good place to start is to incorporate other numbered groupings in the time hand or limbs. Below is the breakdown of the same HH pattern but now utilizing groupings of "3" to create an "over the bar" rhythm. Take note that it takes 3 full measures to come back around to the downbeat of 1 again.

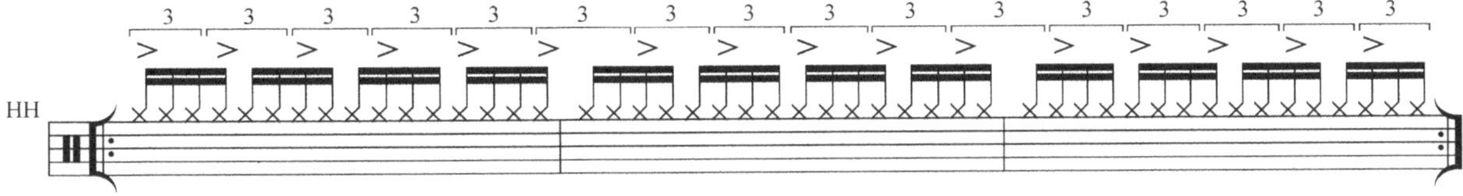

Tip: Counting Exercise

A good suggested exercise for any cross rhythm is to count out loud even before playing as to help build the two existing rhythms internally. Below, you will find a standard 3 measure phrase consisting of only 16th note counts, but every 3rd symbol is in **bold** as to represent the placement of an accent. Start by counting out loud, accentuating the bolded symbols while tapping your foot on downbeats in 4/4:

| **1** e + **a** 2 e **+** a 3 **e** +a **4** e + **a** | 1 e **+** a 2 **e** + a **3** e + **a** 4 e **+** a | 1 **e** +a **2** e+ **a** 3 e **+** a 4 **e** +a |

Primary Ostinato

The following pattern you see is the primary hand ostinato which will remain constant through the various grooves & exercises in this section. As your starting point, practice just this hand pattern together to develop independence involved in keeping the accents in groupings of "3" consistent over the top of the snare drum which remains on 2 & 4 throughout.

Practice Note: To obtain the most successful sound & feel of this ostinato, make sure that you are incorporating a repetitive 3-stroke Moeller accent technique in your time hand while you retain a consistent backbeat technique in the snare hand. Make an effort to ensure that the shifting accents do not affect or change the motion in either hand.

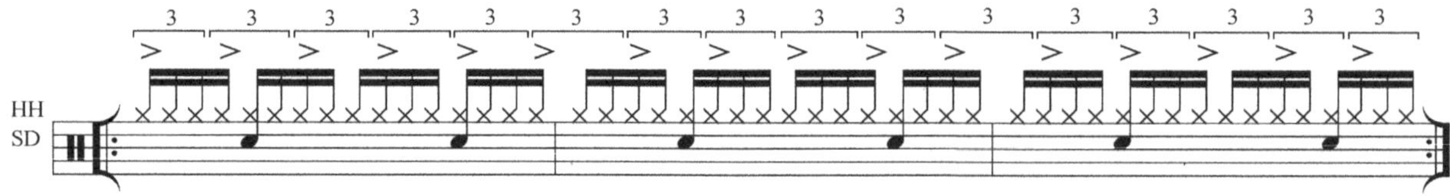

Incorporating the Bass Drum

The final goal is to now complete your phrases & grooves by adding countless bass drum rhythms to the ostinato. A great place to begin is to utilize any beginner drum set book with easy single-measure grooves. Since the full ostinato pattern with the groupings of "3" over the top is 3 measures long, you will need to play the single-measure grooves for 3 measures. Then, add an accent every 3 notes over the top of your HH pattern for everything to line up properly. Here is a starting point, using a "standard groove:"

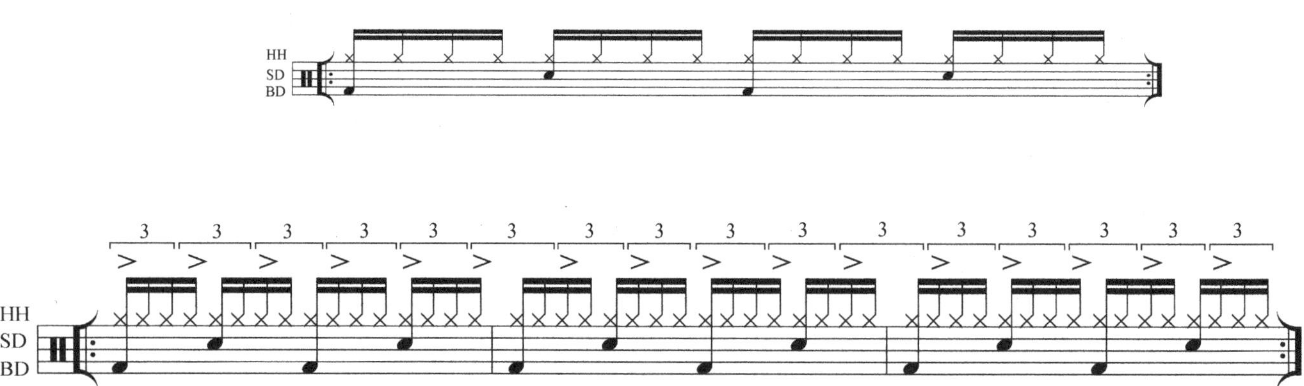

Exercise 13: Basic Beats

16th note rate grooves with groupings of 3 (3/16)

Below, you will find the transcription of the current ostinato once again. The rest of the page contains variations of simple grooves for bass drum variations. There are 3 ways you can go about working on these exercise pages for independence & variation development:

1) On a separate piece of paper, write out the ostinato 12 times. Extract the bass drum notes from the 12 single-measure grooves below and insert them into the ostinato phrases you've transcribed.

2) Play the single-measure phrases 3 times each and insert the accents (by ear) over the top of the grooves you are playing.

3) If you have a physical copy of the book, simply pencil in a bass drum pattern from a single-measure phrase into the ostinato. Once comfortable, erase and then move to transcribing the next patterns down the page one-by-one.

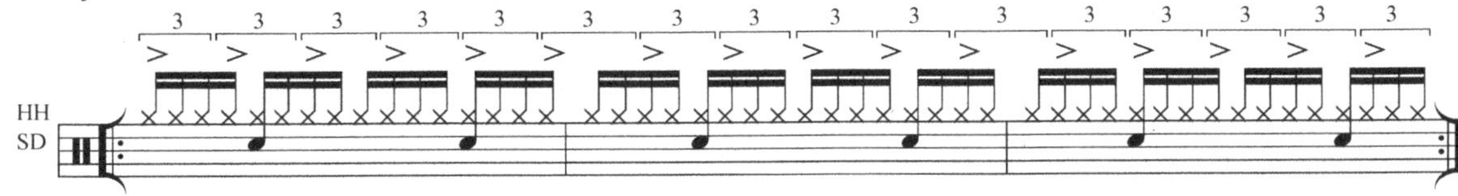

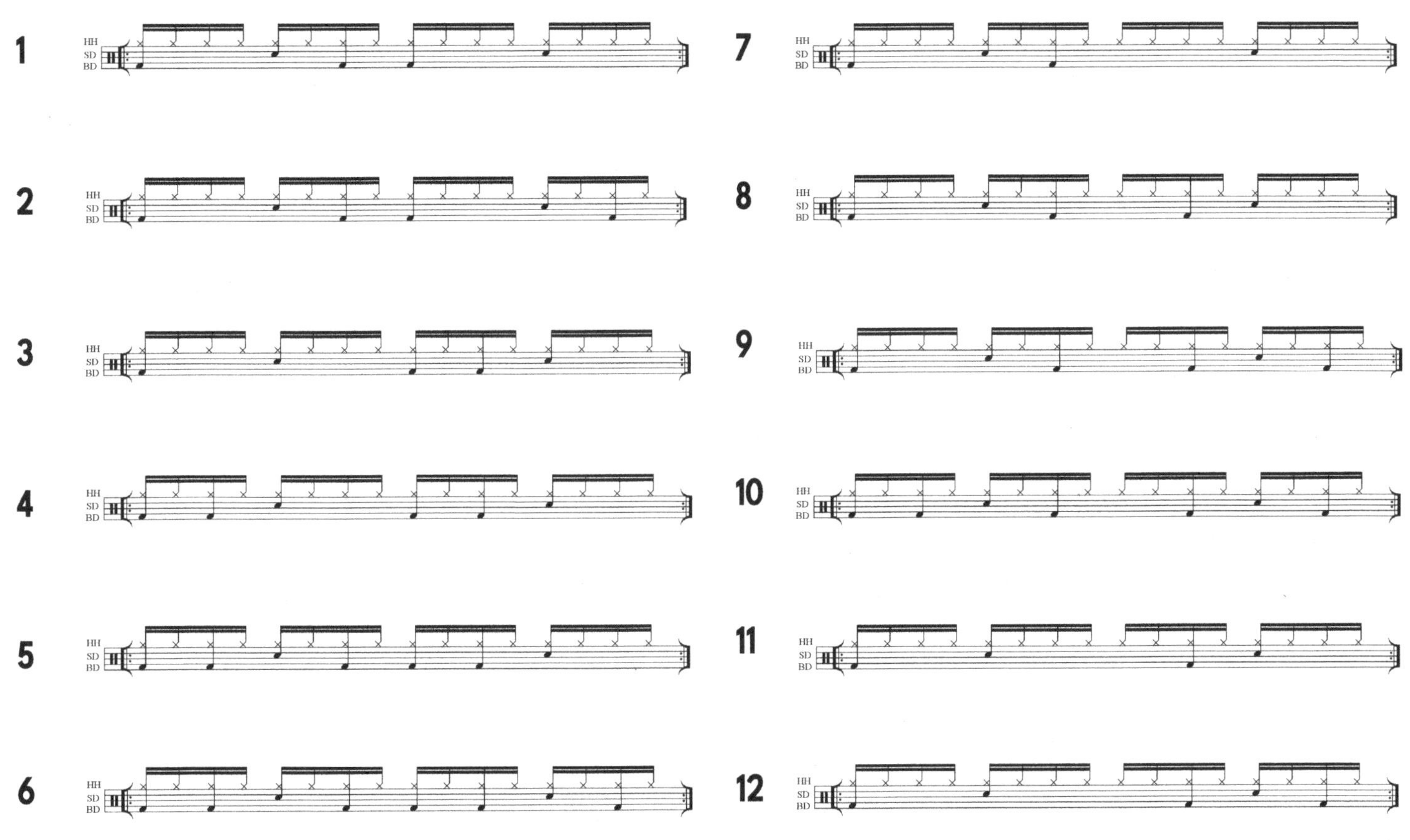

Incorporating a Syncopated Bass Drum Moving Melody

Part 1: Quarter Notes and 8th Notes

The next step in varying your bass drum would be to combine an individual syncopated ongoing melody with the current 16th note ostinato. The melody you will see in the next section is written as if it were a snare melody, but you have the option of applying it to any limb that is applied to the kit. For the current exercises, we will be applying it to or playing it on the bass drum. The most appropriate book to use in this current rhythmic category is *Syncopation for the Modern Drummer* by Ted Reed. The full melody is an example of a page you will find in that book.

Below, find the example of line 1 of the syncopated exercise (found on the next page) and how it is then applied to the bass drum under the current ostinato with groupings of "3." Notice how you're only seeing the first 3 measures of the full melody exercise. Keep in mind that, as in the past few pages, ostinatos containing groupings of "3" will only create 3 bar phrases total in order to come back to your starting point again. Here is an illustration of the combination process, putting the hand pattern and the bass drum melody together.

NOTE: Keep in mind this is the same syncopated melody used in previous pages, but used in conjunction with a 16th note based ostinato, it creates a varied form of independence.

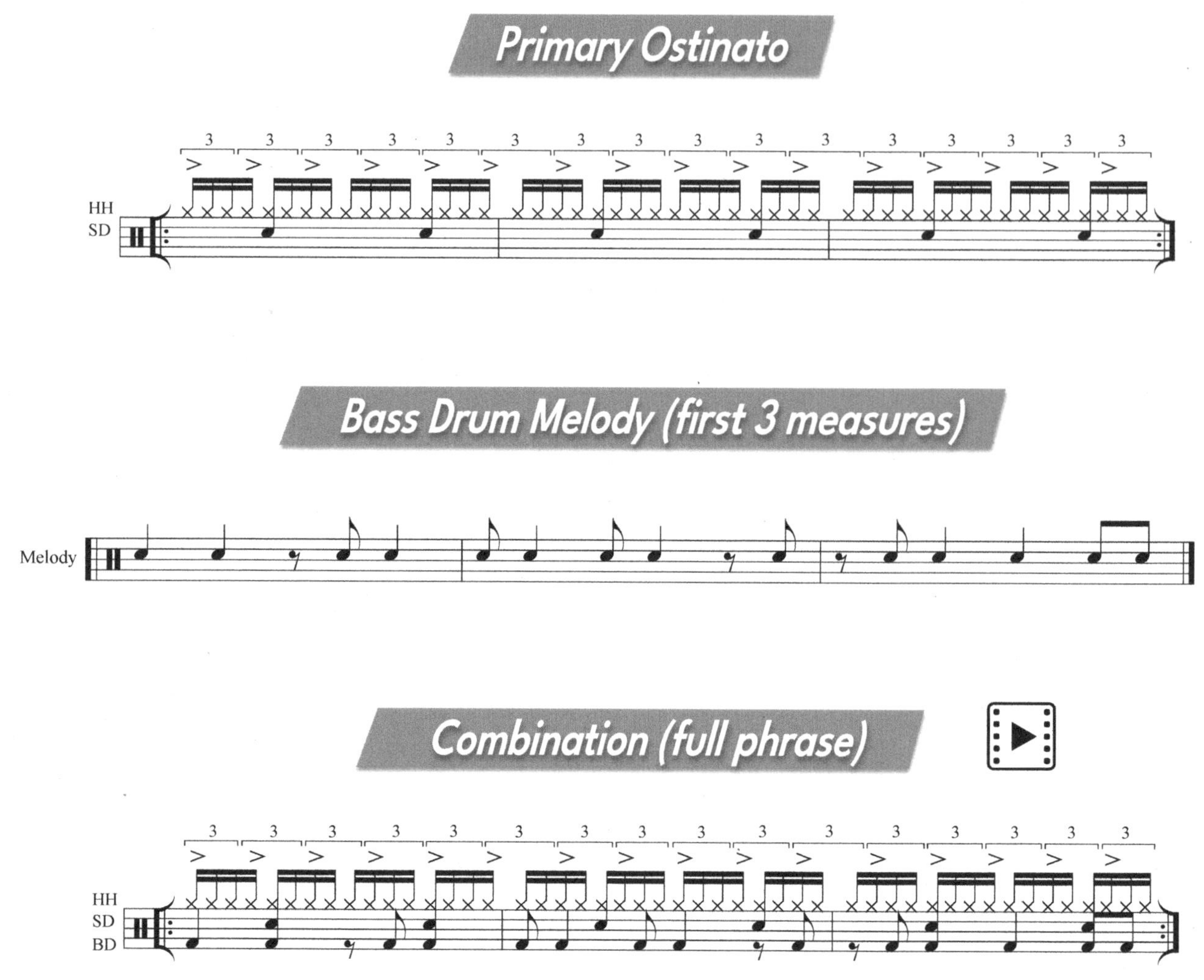

Exercise 14 : Syncopated Moving Melody with Quarters and 8ths

16th note rate grooves with groupings of 3 (3/16)

Below, you will find the transcription of the current ostinato once again. The rest of the page contains the entire rhythmic melody that will be applied to the bass drum. There are 3 ways you can go about working on these exercise pages for independence & variation development:

1) On a separate piece of paper, write out the ostinato 8 times. Insert the bass drum notes from the melody below into the ostinato phrases you've transcribed.

2) Play down the whole exercise/melody and insert the accents (by ear) over the top of the exercise you are playing.

3) If you have a physical copy of the book, simply pencil in 16th notes over the top of the melody and then write in an accent over every 3rd 16th note.

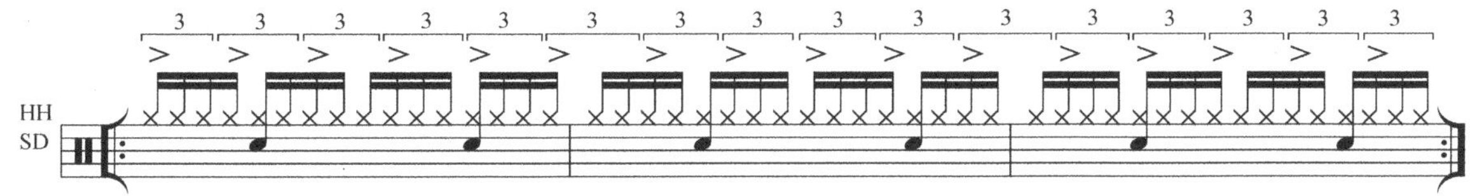

*Asterisks designate the measures where the accented groupings & phrases of "3" will reset on beat 1 again

Incorporating a Syncopated Bass Drum Moving Melody

Part 2: Quarter Notes, 8th Notes and 16th Notes

Furthering your independence in varying your bass drum, the next step would be to incorporate variations of 16th notes within the ongoing melody and then combing that with the current ostinato. The melody you will see in the next section is written as if it were a snare melody, but you have the option of applying it to any limb that is applied to the kit. As with the previous exercises, we will be applying it to or playing it on the bass drum. The most appropriate book to use in this current rhythmic category is *The New Breed* by Gary Chester. The full melody in this section is an example of a page you will find in that book.

Below, find the example of line 1 of the exercise (found on the next page) and how it is then applied to the bass drum under the current ostinato with groupings of "3." Notice how you're only seeing the first 3 measures of the full melody exercise. Keep in mind that, as in the past few pages, ostinatos containing groupings of "3" will only create 3 bar phrases total in order to come back to your starting point again. Here is an illustration of the combination process, putting the hand pattern and the bass drum melody together.

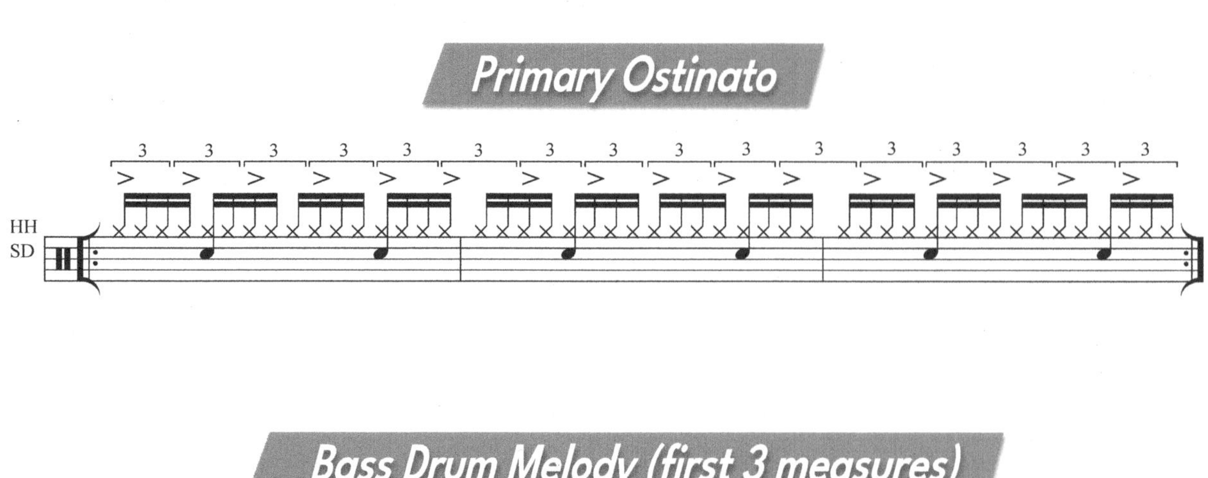

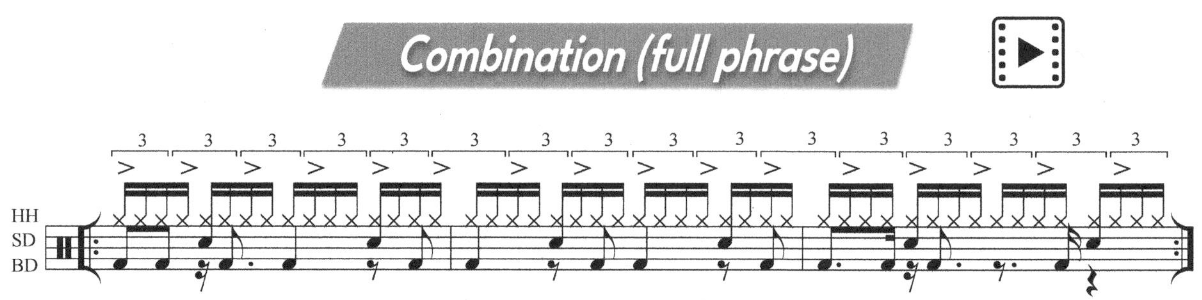

Exercise 15: Syncopated Moving Melody with Quarter Notes, 8th Notes and 16th Notes

16th note rate grooves with groupings of 3 (3/16)

Below, you will find the transcription of the current ostinato once again. The rest of the page contains the entire rhythmic melody that will be applied to the bass drum. There are 3 ways you can go about working on these exercise pages for independence & variation development:

1) On a separate piece of paper, write out the ostinato 8 times. Insert the bass drum notes from the melody below into the ostinato phrases you've transcribed.

2) Play down the whole exercise/melody and insert the accents (by ear) over the top of the exercise you are playing.

3) If you have a physical copy of the book, simply pencil in 16th notes over the top of the melody and then write in an accent over every 3rd 16th note.

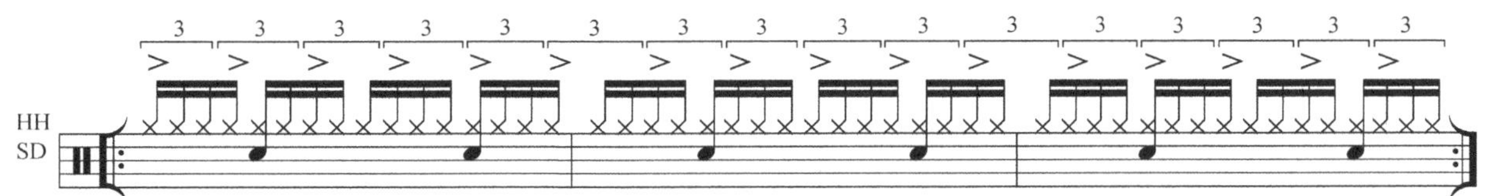

Asterisks designate the measures where the accented groupings & phrases of "3" will reset on beat 1 again

Section 2: Groupings of 5 (5/16 over 4/4)

Following the sequence of the previous chapter, after you feel comfortable working with groupings of "3" in your time hand, a sensible step is to move toward groupings of "5." Below is the breakdown of the HH pattern but now utilizing groupings of "5" to create a larger "over the bar" rhythm. Keep in mind that it now takes 5 full measures to come back around to the downbeat of 1 again.

***Note*:** There are several ways to play or perform the accents in groupings of "5." Playing one accent every 5 notes is a standard approach. However, it's often more musical and/or pleasing to the ear to subdivide the groupings such as a 2+3 or 3+2 phrasing. For practicality & musical purposes, the phrases you see will be organized with a 2+3 phrasing.

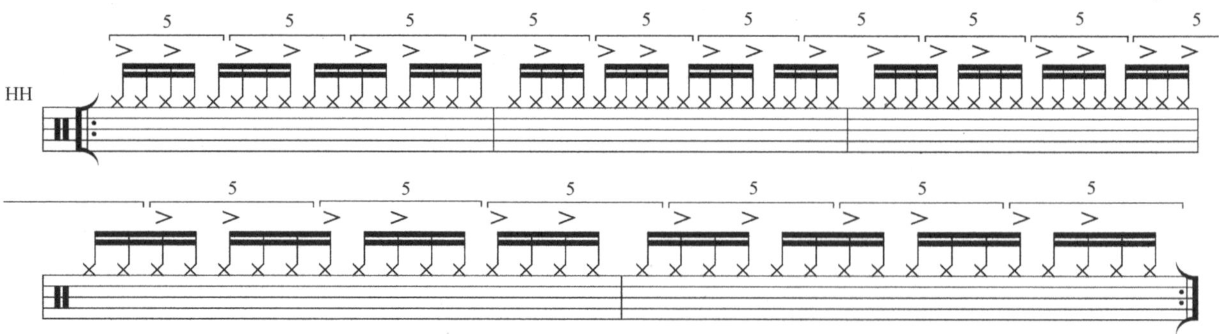

Tip: Counting Exercise

Remember that a good suggested exercise for any cross rhythm is to count out loud even before playing as to help build the two existing rhythms internally. Below, you will find a standard 5 measure phrase consisting of only 16th note counts, but every **bolded** number or symbol represents the placement of an accent. This time, the bolded counts reflect the 2+3 subdivided phrase listed above. Start by counting out loud, accentuating the bolded symbols while tapping your foot on downbeats in 4/4:

| **1** e **+** a 2 **e** + **a** 3 e **+** a **4** e + **a** | 1 **e** +a **2** e **+** a 3 **e** + **a** 4 e **+** a | **1** e+ **a** 2 **e** +a **3** e **+** a 4 **e** + **a** |

| 1 e **+** a **2** e+ **a** 3 **e** +a **4** e **+** a | 1 **e** + **a** 2 e **+** a **3** e+ **a** 4 **e** +a |

The following pattern you see is the primary hand ostinato which will remain constant through the various grooves & exercises in this section. As your starting point, practice just this hand pattern together to develop independence involved in keeping the accents, this time, in groupings of "5," consistent over the top of the snare drum which remains on beats 2 & 4 throughout. Remember that the subdivision break up for your groupings of "5" is a 2+3 phrase.

Practice Note: To obtain the most successful sound & feel of this ostinato, make sure that you are incorporating a repetitive Moeller accent technique in 2 strokes, then 3 strokes, each phrase in your time hand while you retain a consistent backbeat technique in the snare hand. Make an effort to ensure that the shifting accents do not affect or change the motion in either hand.

Primary Ostinato

Introducing the Bass Drum

Similar to the previous section in this chapter, the final goal is to now complete your phrases & grooves by adding countless bass drum rhythms to the ostinato. A great place to begin is to utilize any beginner drum set book with easy single-measure grooves. Since the full ostinato pattern with the groupings of "5" over the top is 5 measures long, you will need to play the single-measure grooves for 5 measures. Then, add the 2+3 phrases of "5" over the top of your HH pattern for everything to line up properly. Here is a starting point, using a "standard groove:"

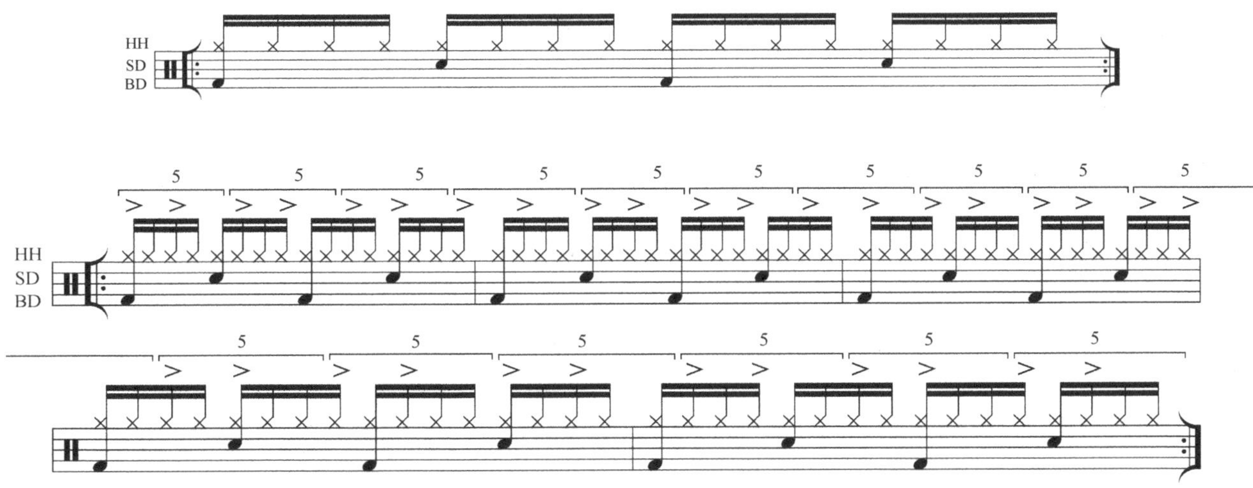

Exercise 16: Basic Beats

16th note rate grooves with groupings of 5 (5/16)

Below, you will find the transcription of the current ostinato once again. The rest of the page contains the same previous variations of simple grooves for bass drum variations. There are 3 ways you can go about working on these exercise pages for independence & variation development:

1) On a separate piece of paper, write out the ostinato 12 times. Extract the bass drum notes from the 12 single-measure grooves below and insert them into the ostinato phrases you've transcribed.

2) Play the single-measure phrases 5 times each and insert the accents (by ear) over the top of the grooves you are playing.

3) If you have a physical copy of the book, simply pencil in a bass drum pattern from a single-measure phrase into the ostinato below. Once comfortable, erase and then move to transcribing the next patterns down the page one-by-one.

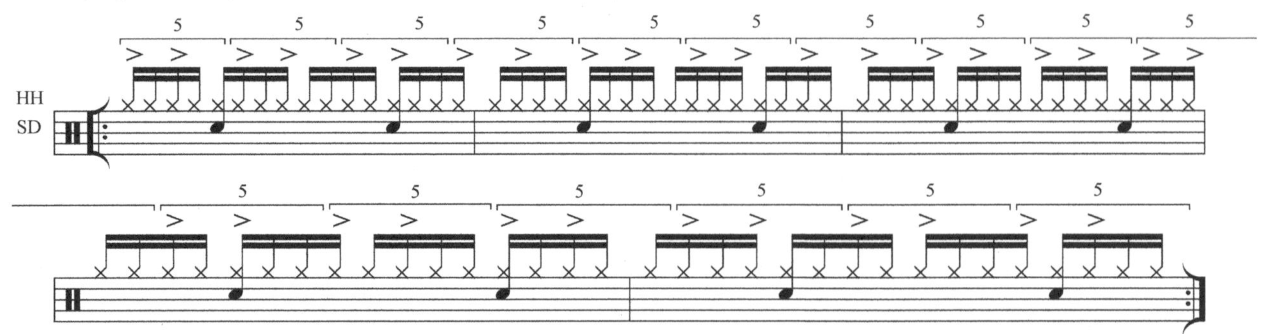

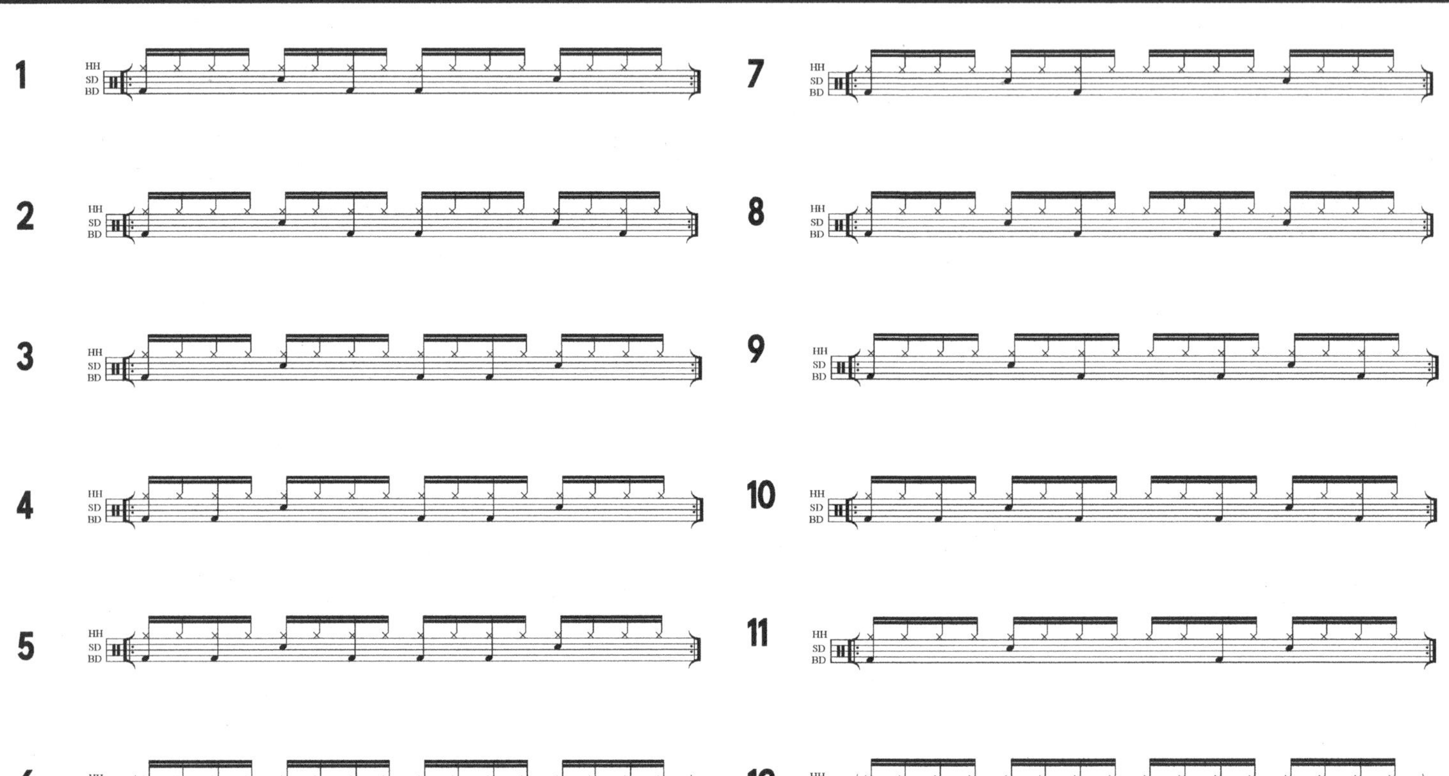

Incorporating a Syncopated Bass Drum Moving Melody

Part 1: Quarter Notes and 8th Notes

The next step in varying your bass drum would be to combine an individual syncopated ongoing melody with the current 16th note ostinato. The melody you will see in the next section is written as if it were a snare melody, but you have the option of applying it to any limb that is applied to the kit. For the current exercises, we will be applying it to or playing it on the bass drum. The most appropriate book to use in this current rhythmic category is 'Syncopation for the Modern Drummer' by Ted Reed. The full melody is an example of a page you will find in that book.

Below, find the example of line 1 of the syncopated exercise (found on the next page) and how it is then applied to the bass drum under the current ostinato with groupings of "5." Notice how you're only seeing the first 5 measures of the full melody exercise. Keep in mind that, as in the past few pages, ostinatos containing groupings of "5" will only create 5 bar phrases total in order to come back to your starting point again. Here is an illustration of the combination process, putting the hand pattern and the bass drum melody together.

NOTE: Keep in mind this is the same syncopated melody used in previous pages, but used in conjunction with a 16th note based ostinato, it creates a varied form of independence.

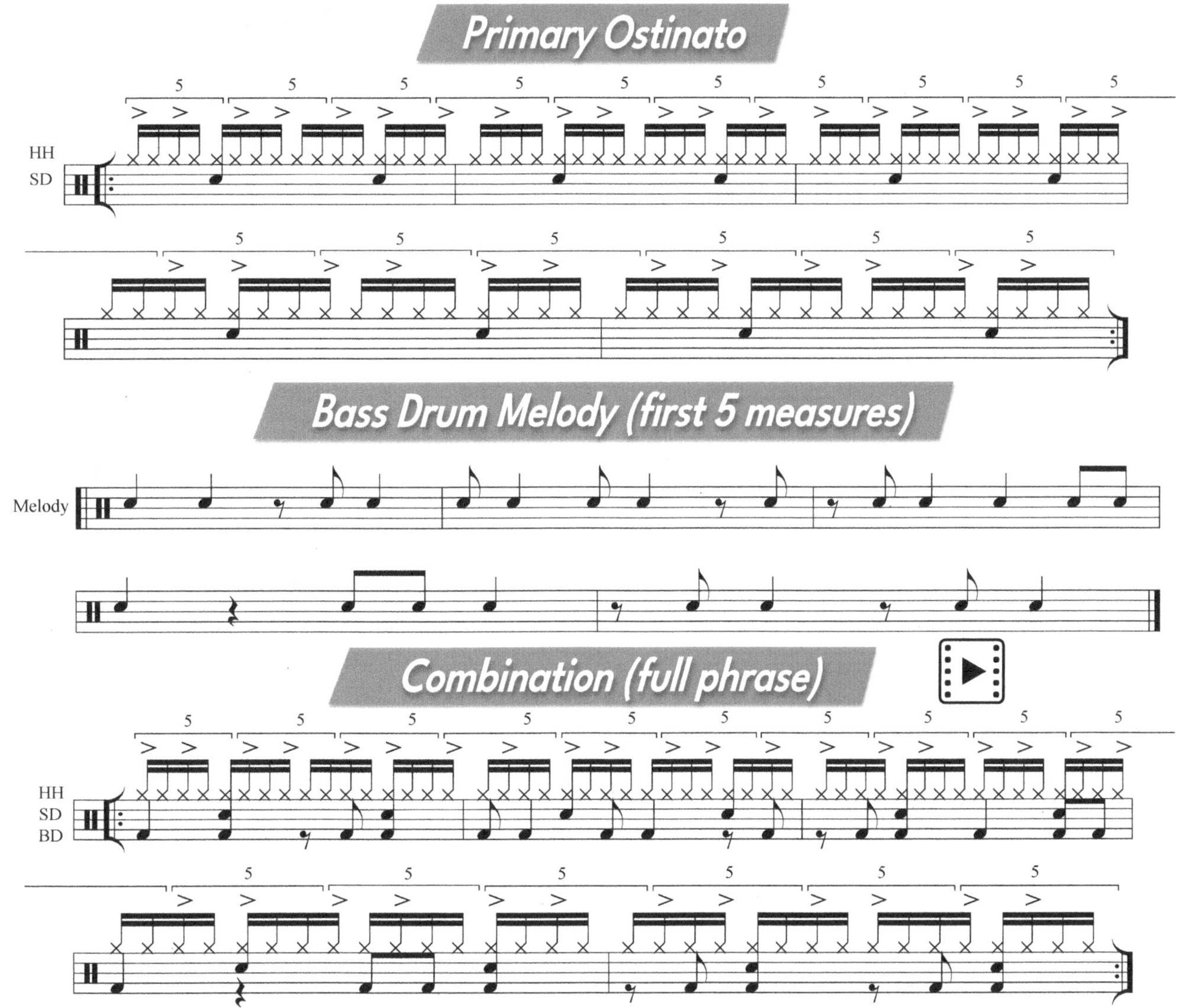

Exercise 17: Syncopated Moving Melody with Quarters and 8ths

16th note rate grooves with groupings of 5 (5/16)

Below, you will find the transcription of the current ostinato once again. The rest of the page contains the entire rhythmic melody that will be applied to the bass drum. There are 3 ways you can go about working on these exercise pages for independence & variation development:

1) On a separate piece of paper, write out the ostinato several times. Insert the bass drum notes from the melody below into the ostinato phrases you've transcribed.

2) Play down the whole exercise/melody and insert the accents (by ear) over the top of the exercise you are playing.

3) If you have a physical copy of the book, simply pencil in 16th notes over the top of the melody and then write in 2+3 groupings over the ongoing 16th notes.

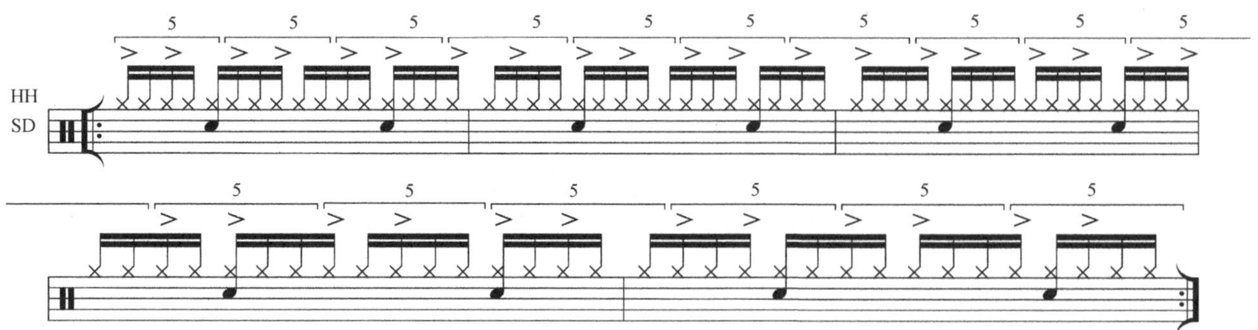

Asterisks designate the measures where the accented groupings & phrases of "5" will reset on beat 1 again

Incorporating a Syncopated Bass Drum Moving Melody

Part 2: Quarter Notes, 8th Notes and 16th Notes

Furthering your independence in varying your bass drum, the next step would be to incorporate variations of 16th notes within the ongoing melody and then combing that with the current ostinato. The melody you will see in the next section is written as if it were a snare melody, but you have the option of applying it to any limb that is applied to the kit. As with the previous exercises, we will be applying it to or playing it on the bass drum. The most appropriate book to use in this current rhythmic category is 'The New Breed' by Gary Chester. The full melody in this section is an example of a page you will find in that book.

Below, find the example of the first 5 measures of the exercise (found on the next page) and how it is then applied to the bass drum under the current ostinato with groupings of "5." Notice how you're only seeing the first 5 measures of the full melody exercise. Keep in mind that, as in the past few pages, ostinatos containing groupings of "5" will only create 5 bar phrases total in order to come back to your starting point again. Here is an illustration of the combination process, putting the hand pattern and the bass drum melody together.

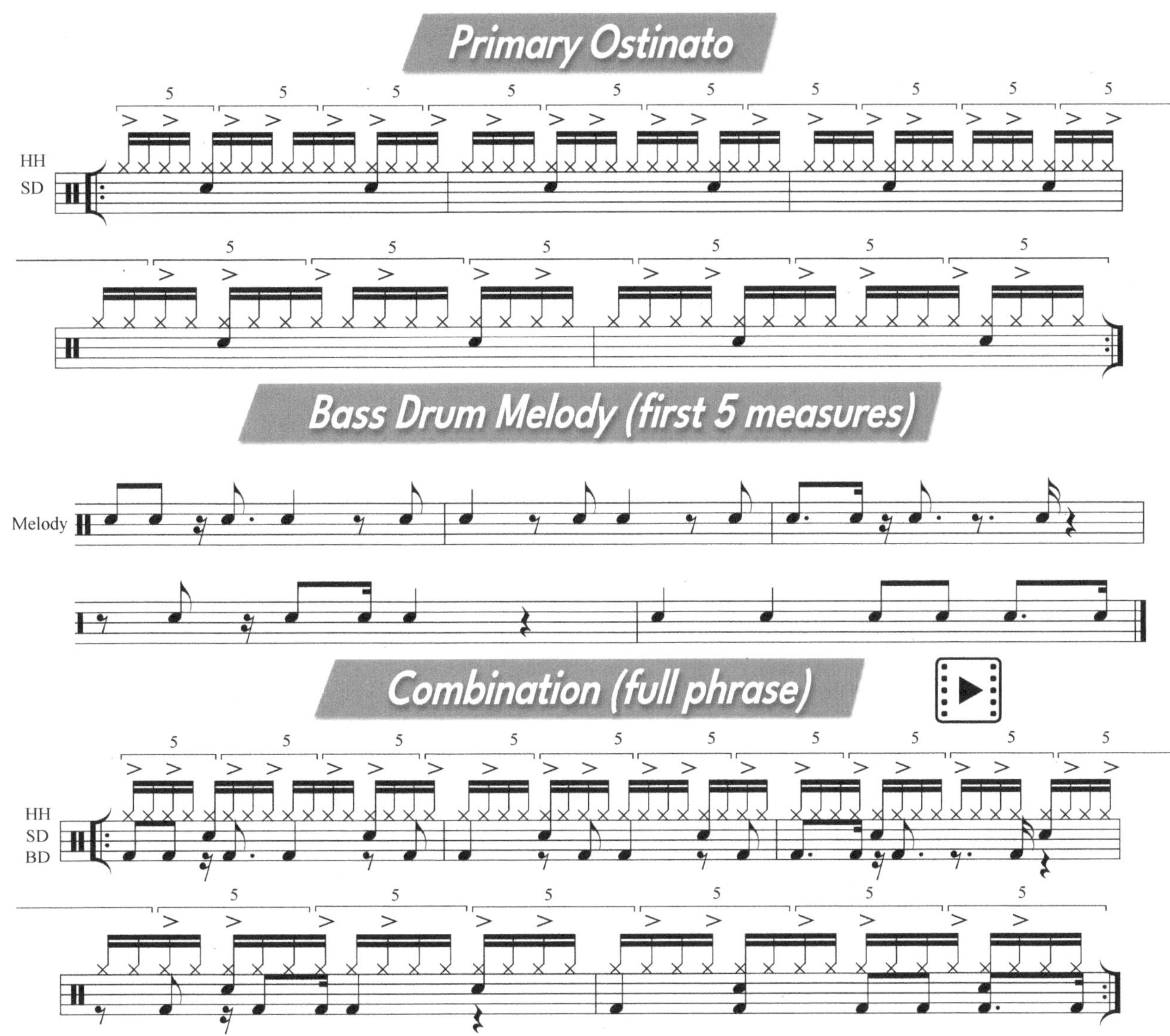

Exercise 18: Syncopated Moving Melody with Quarter Notes, 8th Notes and 16th Notes

16th note rate grooves with groupings of 5 (5/16)

Below, you will find the transcription of the current ostinato once again. The rest of the page contains the entire rhythmic melody that will be applied to the bass drum. There are 3 ways you can go about working on these exercise pages for independence & variation development:

1) On a separate piece of paper, write out the ostinato several times. Insert the bass drum notes from the melody below into the ostinato phrases you've transcribed.

2) Play down the whole exercise/melody and insert the accents (by ear) over the top of the exercise you are playing.

3) If you have a physical copy of the book, simply pencil in 16th notes over the top of the melody and then write in 2+3 groupings over the ongoing 16th notes.

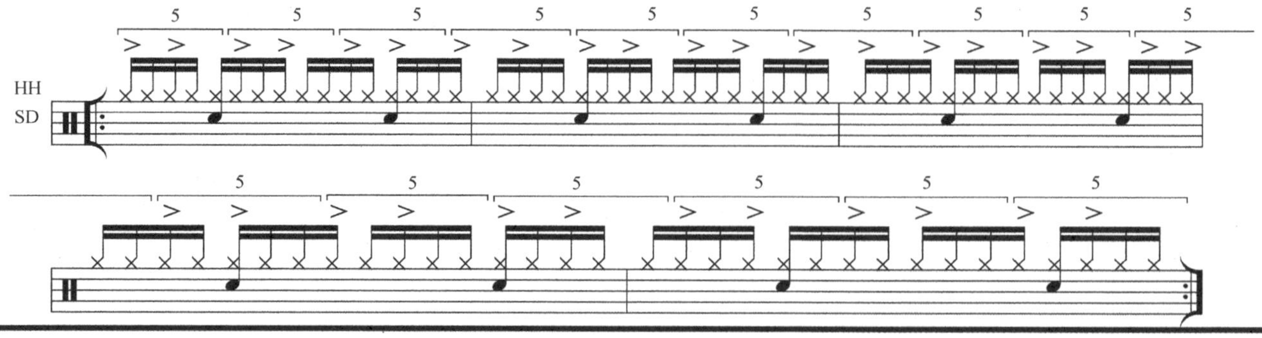

HH
SD

Melody

Asterisks designate the measures where the accented groupings & phrases of "5" will reset on beat 1 again

Section 3: Groupings of 7 (7/16 over 4/4)

Following the sequence of the previous chapter, after you feel comfortable working with groupings of "5" in your time hand, a sensible step is to move toward groupings of "7." Below is the breakdown of the HH pattern but now utilizing groupings of "7" to create a larger "over the bar" rhythm. Keep in mind that it now takes 7 full measures to come back around to the downbeat of 1 again.

***Note*:** There are several ways to play or perform the accents in groupings of "7." Playing one accent every 7 notes is a standard approach. However, it's often more musical and/or pleasing to the ear to subdivide the groupings such as a 2+2+3 or 3+2+2 phrasing (even a 2+3+2 phrasing is used). For practicality & musical purposes, the phrases you see will be organized with a 2+2+3 phrasing.

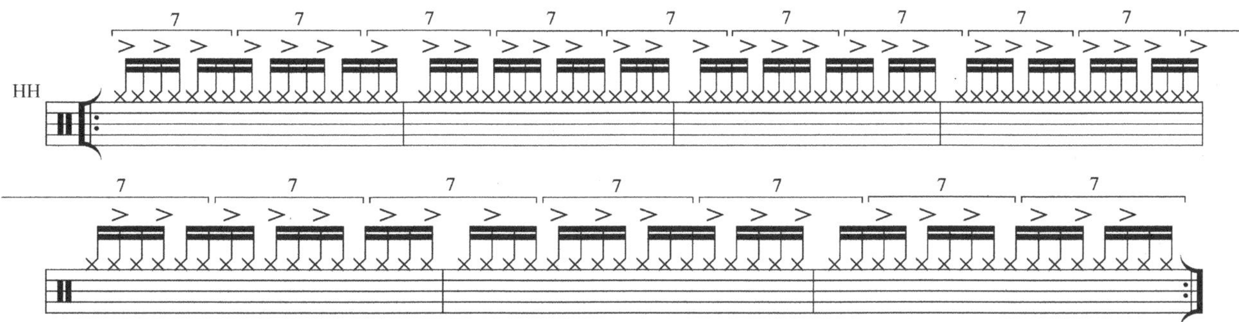

Tip: Counting Exercise

Remember that a good suggested exercise for any cross rhythm is to count out loud even before playing as to help build the two existing rhythms internally. Below, you will find a standard 7 measure phrase consisting of only 16th note counts, but every **bolded** number or symbol represents the placement of an accent. This time, the bolded counts reflect the 2+2+3 subdivided phrase listed above. Start by counting out loud, accentuating the bolded symbols while tapping your foot on downbeats in 4/4:

| **1** e **+** a **2** e + **a** 3 **e** + **a** 4 e **+** a | **1** e **+** a 2 **e** + **a** 3 **e** + a **4** e **+** a | **1** e + **a** 2 **e** + **a** 3 e **+** a **4** e **+** a |

| 1 **e** + **a** 2 **e** + a **3** e **+** a **4** e + **a** | 1 **e** + **a** 2 e **+** a **3** e **+** a 4 **e** + **a** | 1 **e** + a **2** e **+** a **3** e + **a** 4 **e** + **a** |

| 1 e **+** a **2** e **+** a 3 **e** + **a** 4 **e** + a |

Primary Ostinato

The following pattern you see is the primary hand ostinato which will remain constant through the various grooves & exercises in this next section. As your starting point, practice just this hand pattern together to develop independence involved in keeping the accents, this time, in groupings of "7," consistent over the top of the snare drum which remains on beats 2 & 4 throughout. Remember that the subdivision break up for your groupings of "7" is a 2+2+3 phrase.

Practice Note: To obtain the most successful sound & feel of this ostinato, make sure that you are incorporating a repetitive Moeller accent technique in 2 strokes, then 2 strokes, then 3 strokes, each phrase in your time hand while you retain a consistent backbeat technique in the snare hand. Make an effort to ensure that the shifting accents do not affect or change the motion in either hand.

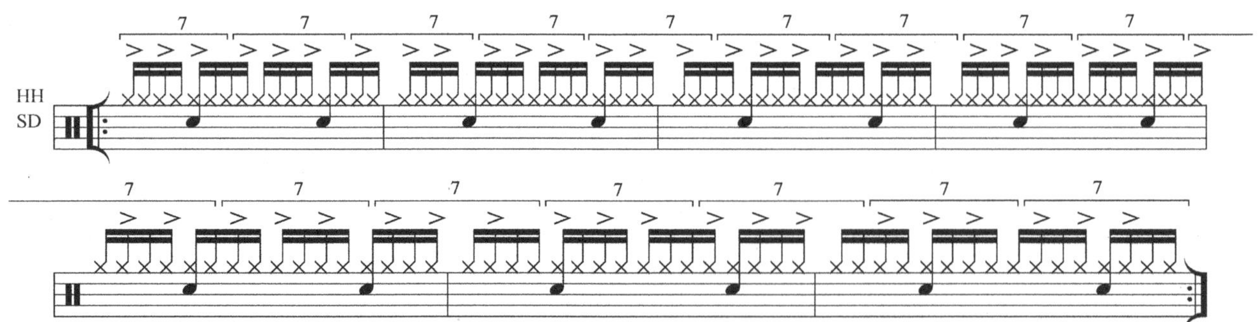

Incorporating the Bass Drum

Similar to the previous sections in this chapter, the final goal is to now complete your phrases & grooves by adding countless bass drum rhythms to the ostinato. A great place to begin is to utilize any beginner drum set book with easy single-measure grooves. Since the full ostinato pattern with the groupings of "7" over the top is 7 measures long, you will need to play the single-measure grooves for 7 measures. Then, add the 2+2+3 phrases of "7" over the top of your HH pattern for everything to line up properly. Here is a starting point, using a "standard groove:"

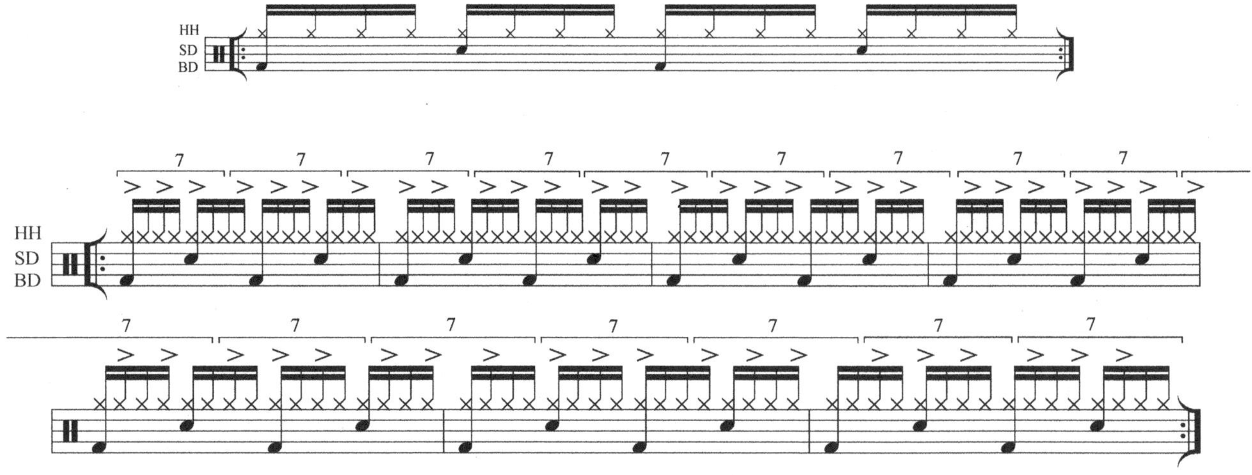

Exercise 19: Basic Beats

16th note rate grooves with groupings of 7 (7/16)

Below, you will find the transcription of the current ostinato once again. The rest of the page contains variations of simple grooves for bass drum variations. There are 3 ways you can go about working on these exercise pages for independence & variation development:

1) On a separate piece of paper, write out the ostinato 12 times. Extract the bass drum notes from the 12 single-measure grooves below and insert them into the ostinato phrases you've transcribed.

2) Play the single-measure phrases 7 times each and insert the accents (by ear) over the top of the grooves you are playing.

3) If you have a physical copy of the book, simply pencil in a bass drum pattern from a single-measure phrase into the ostinato below. Once comfortable, erase and then move to transcribing the next patterns down the page one-by-one.

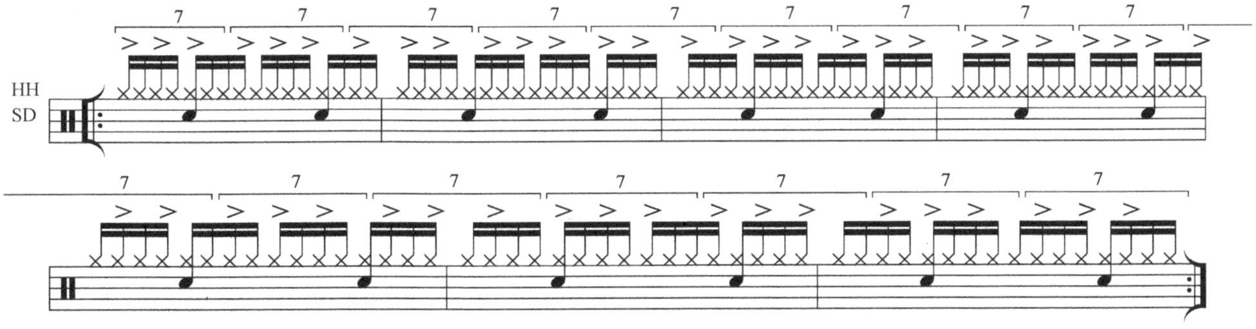

HH
SD

1

2

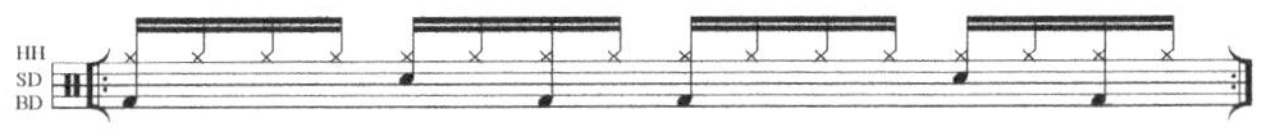

3

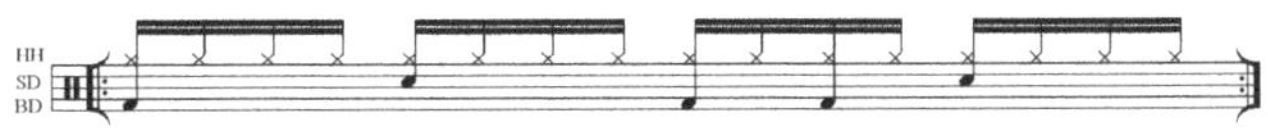

4

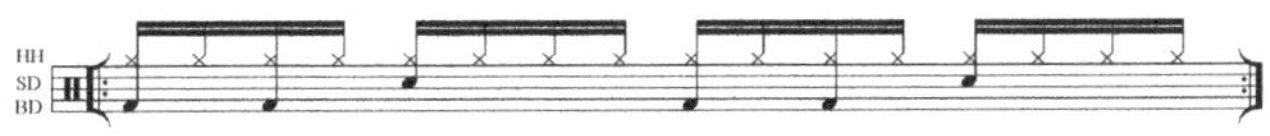

5

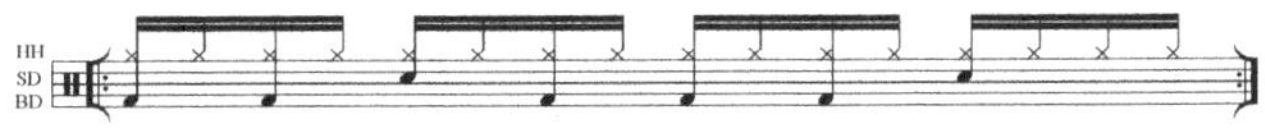

6

7

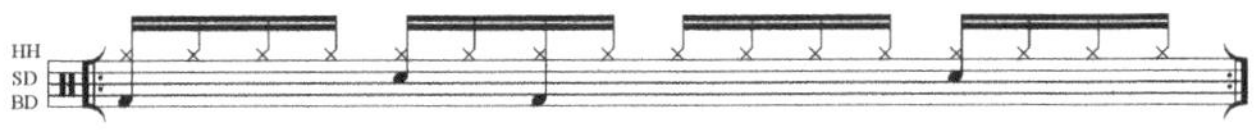

8

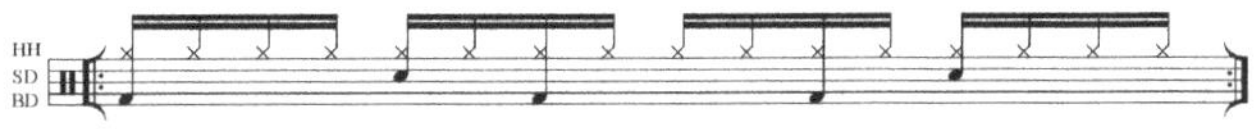

9

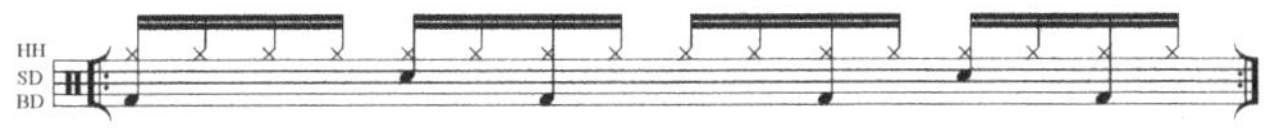

10

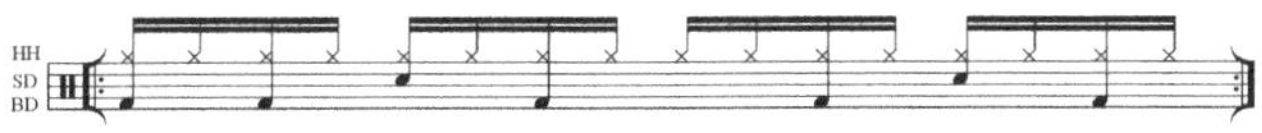

11

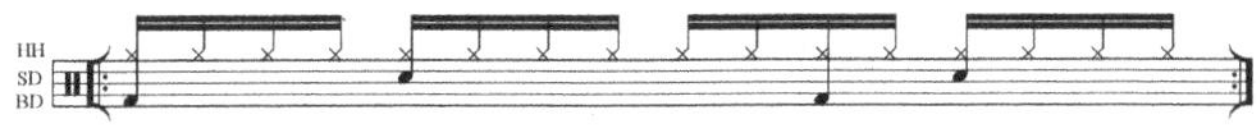

12

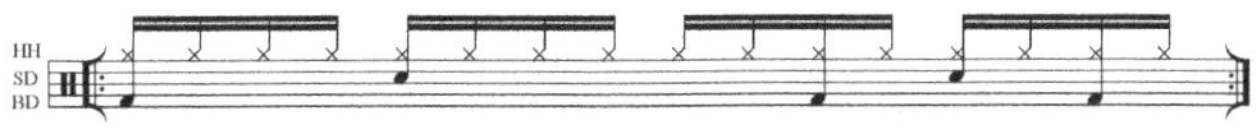

Incorporating a Syncopated Bass Drum Moving Melody

Part 1: Quarter Notes and 8th Notes

The next step in varying your bass drum would be to combine an individual syncopated ongoing melody with the current ostinato. The melody you will see in the next section is written as if it were a snare melody, but you have the option of applying it to any limb that is applied to the kit. For the current exercises, we will be applying it to or playing it on the bass drum. The most appropriate book to use in this current rhythmic category is *Syncopation for the Modern Drummer* by Ted Reed. The full melody is an example of a page you will find in that book.

Below, find the first 7 measures of the syncopated exercise (found on the next page) and how it is then applied to the bass drum under the current ostinato with groupings of "7." Notice how you're only seeing the first 7 measures of the full melody exercise. Keep in mind that, as in the past few pages, ostinatos containing groupings of "7" will create 7 bar phrases total in order to come back to your starting point again. Here is an illustration of the combination process, putting the hand pattern and the bass drum melody together.

NOTE: Keep in mind this is the same syncopated melody used in previous pages, but used in conjunction with a 16th note based ostinato, it creates a varied form of independence.

Primary Ostinato

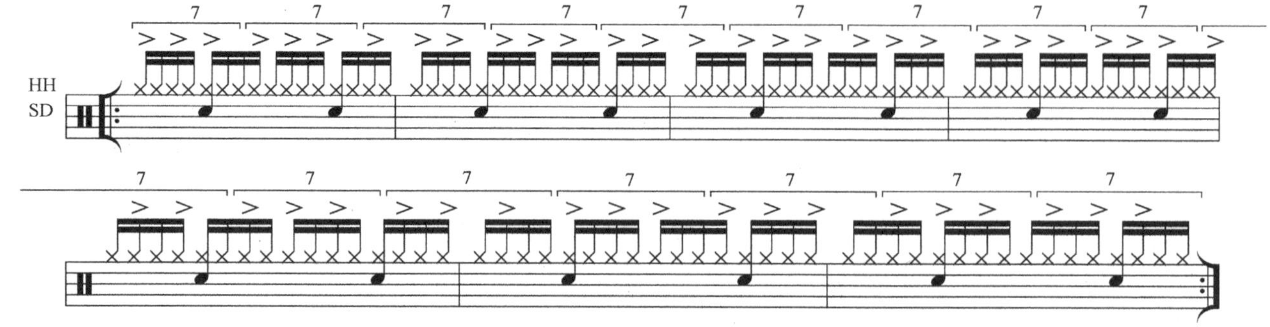

Bass Drum Melody (first 7 measures)

Combination (full phrase)

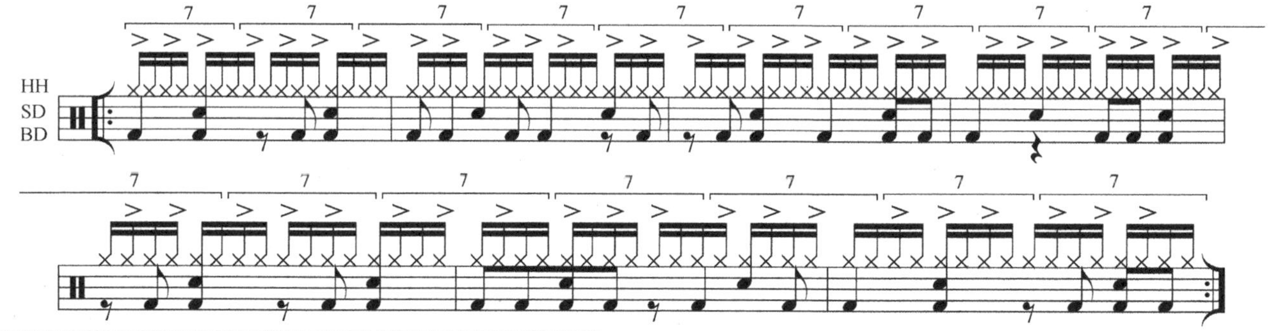

Exercise 20: Syncopated Moving Melody with Quarters and 8ths

16th note rate grooves with groupings of 7 (7/16)

Below, you will find the transcription of the current ostinato once again. The rest of the page contains the entire rhythmic melody that will be applied to the bass drum. There are 3 ways you can go about working on these exercise pages for independence & variation development:

1) On a separate piece of paper, write out the ostinato several times. Insert the bass drum notes from the melody below into the ostinato phrases you've transcribed.

2) Play down the whole exercise/melody and insert the accents (by ear) over the top of the exercise you are playing.

3) If you have a physical copy of the book, simply pencil in 16th notes over the top of the melody and then write in 2+2+3 groupings over the ongoing 16th notes.

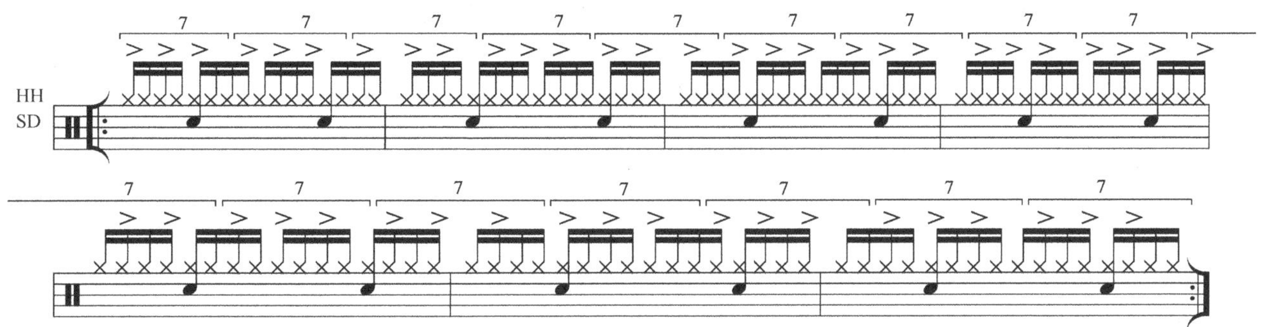

Asterisks designate the measures where the accented groupings & phrases of "7" will reset on beat 1 again

Incorporating a Syncopated Bass Drum Moving Melody

Part 2: Quarter Notes, 8th Notes and 16th Notes

Furthering your independence in varying your bass drum, the next step would be to incorporate variations of 16th notes within the ongoing melody and then combining that with the current ostinato. The melody you will see in the next section is written as if it were a snare melody, but you have the option of applying it to any limb that is applied to the kit. As with the previous exercises, we will be applying it to or playing it on the bass drum. The most appropriate book to use in this current rhythmic category is *The New Breed* by Gary Chester. The full melody in this section is an example of a page you will find in that book.

Below, find the first 7 measures of the exercise (found on the next page) and how it is then applied to the bass drum under the current ostinato with groupings of "7." Notice how you're only seeing the first 7 measures of the full melody exercise. Keep in mind that, as in the past few pages, ostinatos containing groupings of "7" will create 7 bar phrases total in order to come back to your starting point again. Here is an illustration of the combination process, putting the hand pattern and the bass drum melody together.

Primary Ostinato

HH
SD

Bass Drum Melody (first 7 measures)

Melody

Combination (full phrase)

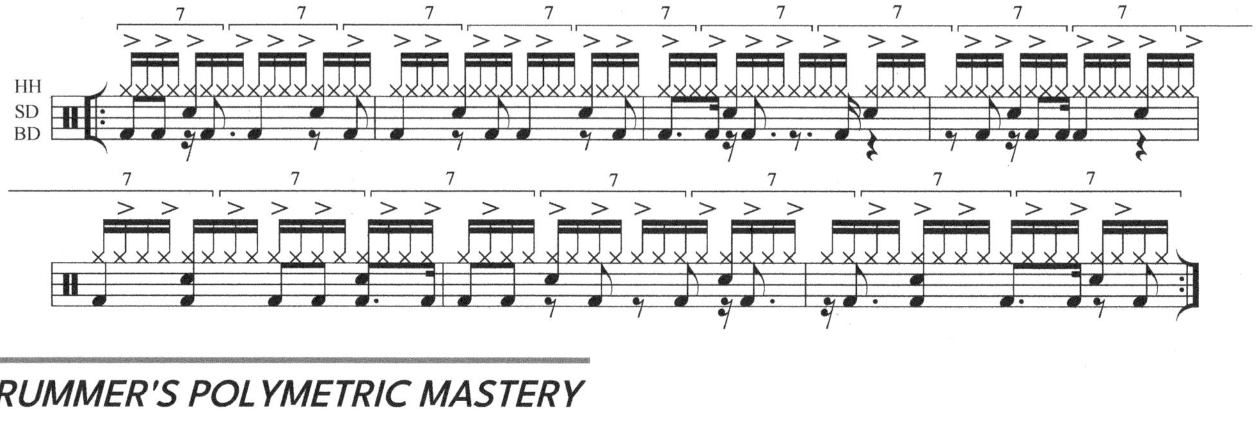

HH
SD
BD

Exercise 21 : Syncopated Moving Melody with Quarter Notes, 8th Notes and 16th Notes

16th note rate grooves with groupings of 7 (7/16)

Below, you will find the transcription of the current ostinato once again. The rest of the page contains the entire rhythmic melody that will be applied to the bass drum. There are 3 ways you can go about working on these exercise pages for independence & variation development:

1) On a separate piece of paper, write out the ostinato several times. Insert the bass drum notes from the melody below into the ostinato phrases you've transcribed.

2) Play down the whole exercise/melody and insert the accents (by ear) over the top of the exercise you are playing.

3) If you have a physical copy of the book, simply pencil in 16th notes over the top of the melody and then write in 2+2+3 groupings over the ongoing 16th notes.

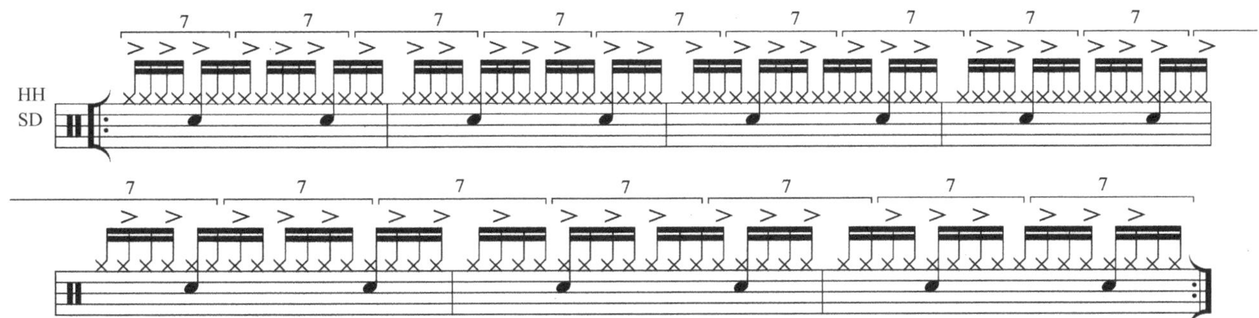

Asterisks designate the measures where the accented groupings & phrases of "7" will reset on beat 1 again

AMAHA
ROCK AGES
JARRETT KRAUSS
2011-2013

YAMAHA
ULTIMATE

HH
SD
BD

Roland

CREW

Section 4: Groove Displacement

Though the ostinatos have presented their own challenges with displacement or movement of "time," notice that the previous exercises throughout the chapter have been only inclusive of a standard groove or backbeat on 2 & 4 from the snare drum. To round out the material in this chapter, a challenging set of exercises centers around using the current ostinatos but now "assigning" the snare drum and bass drum to specific beats in order to cover the topic of ***displacement***. ***NOTE:*** This portion of the chapter reflects the same concepts at the end of Chapter 1, but now incorporates the usage of the 16th note rate.

Before attempting to jump into the polymetric combinations of rhythms, below is the explanation of a practical displacement method in a standard 4/4 meter with no cross rhythms.

Note: The primary suggested exercises throughout this next section use only the current syncopated moving melody of quarter note, 8th note and 16th notes that has appeared on previous pages.

"Boxed-Off" Melody

In order to start assigning the bass drum & snare drum to proper beats, a good first step is to "box off" the melody so you can clearly see where beats 1, 2, 3 & 4 are located.

Development of Full Displaced Groove

Finally, play the bass drum & snare drum in their proper places by sticking with standard groove rules: Anything falling inside the boxes of 1 & 3 will be played on the bass drum; anything falling inside the boxes of 2 & 4 will be played on the snare drum. Shown below is the completed groove with the addition of standard HH 16th notes (with accents every other stroke) along with the bass drum & snare drum on their respective staff lines.

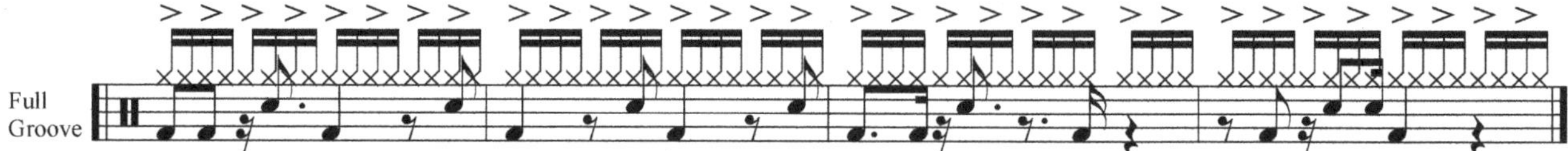

Incorporating the Ostinatos With the Displacement Method

Once you are comfortable with the process of assigning & displacing the melody onto the proper surfaces, the next step would be to apply the polymetric ostinatos to the exercises. Below, you will find a brief example each of the previous ostinatos combined with the process of displacement.

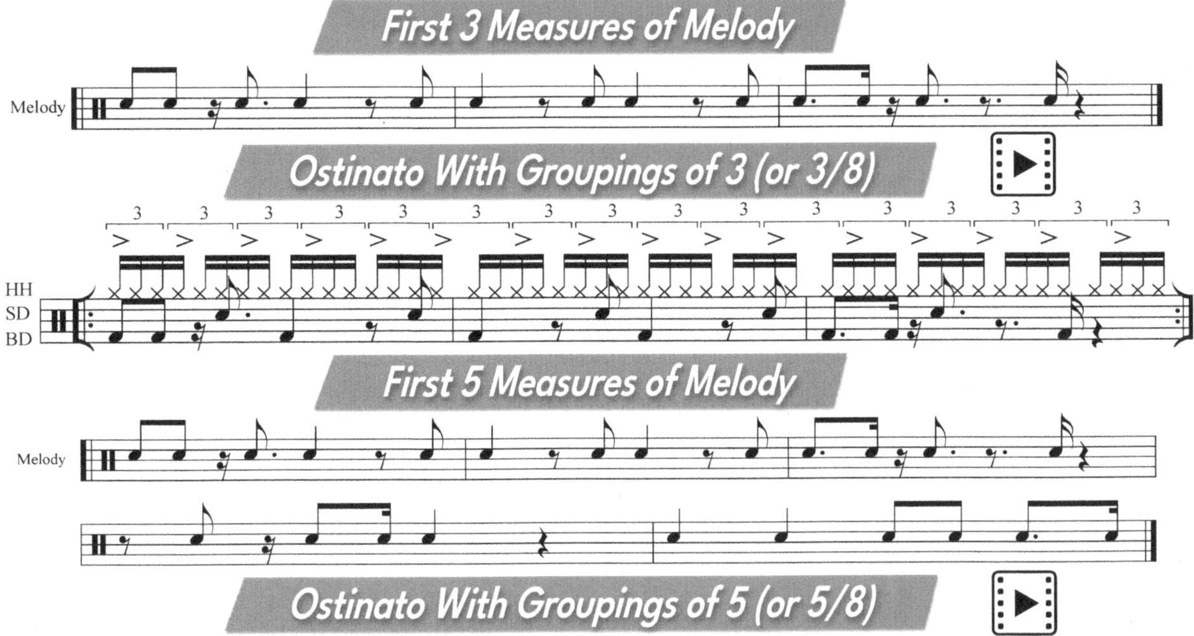

Here is the example of the melody displacement method combined with the ostinato with groupings of "5."
NOTE: You're only seeing the first 5 measures of the melody due to the phrase resetting after 5 measures.

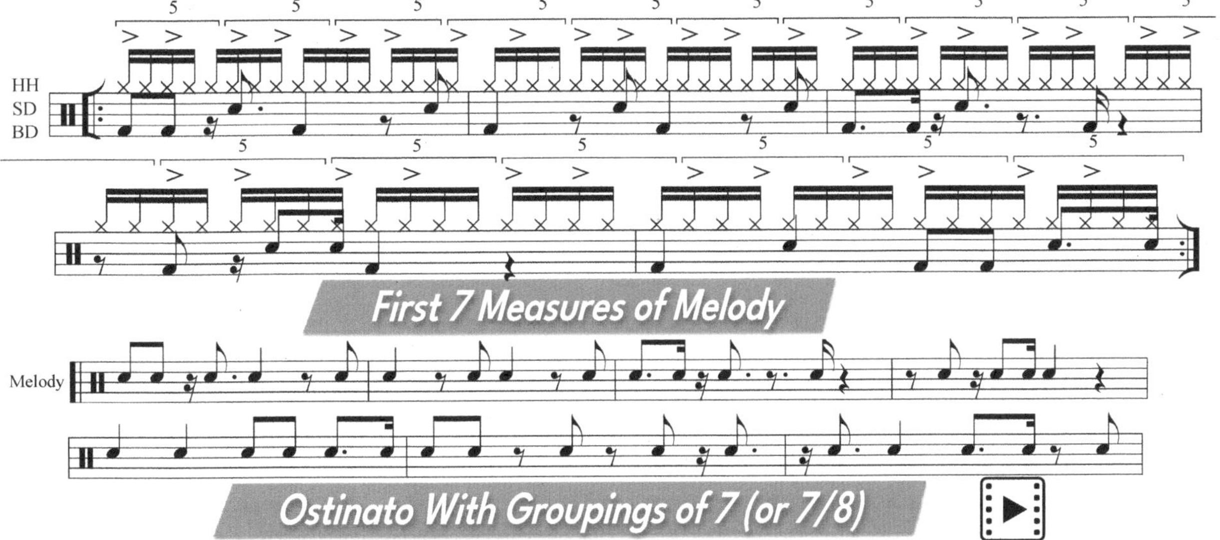

Here is the example of the melody displacement method combined with the ostinato with groupings of "7."
NOTE: You're only seeing the first 7 measures of the melody due to the phrase resetting after 7 measures.

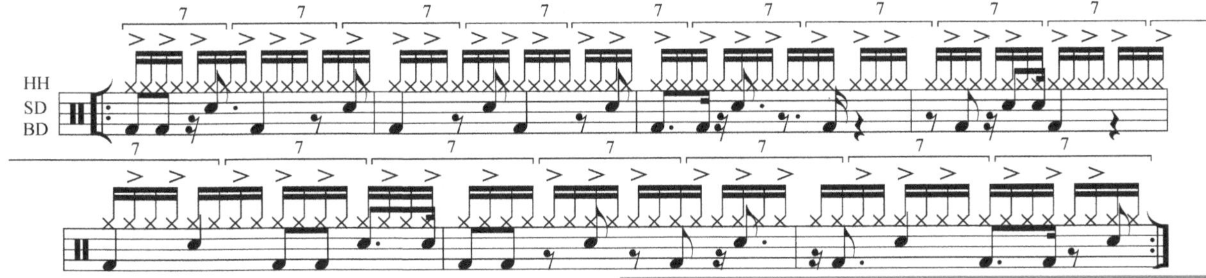

Exercise 22: Incorporating Displaced Moving Melody With the Ostinato

16th note rate grooves with groupings of 3 (3/16)

Below, you will find transcription of the ostinato containing groupings of "3." However, this time, only the HH is included. Since the assignment utilizes movement of both bass drum & snare drum, the only constant pattern are the accents in the HH hand. The rest of the page contains the entire rhythmic melody that will be altered by assigning the bass drum & snare drum on the proper counts. There are 3 ways you can go about working on these exercise pages for independence & variation development:

1) On a separate piece of paper, write out the ostinato 8 times. Insert the assigned bass drum & snare drum notes from the melody below into the ostinato phrases you've transcribed.

2) Play down the whole exercise/melody and insert the accents (by ear) over the top of the exercise you are playing.

3) If you have a physical copy of the book, simply pencil in 16th notes over the top of the melody and then write in an accent over every 3rd 16th note.

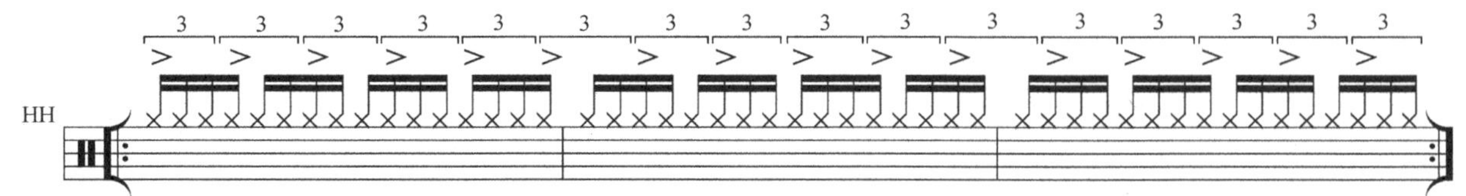

**Asterisks designate the measures where the accented groupings & phrases of "3" will reset on beat 1 again*

Exercise 23: Incorporating Displaced Moving Melody With the Ostinato

16th note rate grooves with groupings of 5 (5/16)

Below, you will find a transcription of the ostinato containing groupings of "5." However, this time, only the HH is included. Since the assignment utilizes movement of both bass drum & snare drum, the only constant pattern are the accents in the HH hand. The rest of the page contains the entire rhythmic melody that will be altered by assigning the bass drum & snare drum on the proper counts. There are 3 ways you can go about working on these exercise pages for independence & variation development:

1) On a separate piece of paper, write out the ostinato several times. Insert the assigned bass drum & snare drum notes from the melody below into the ostinato phrases you've transcribed.

2) Play down the whole exercise/melody and insert the accents (by ear) over the top of the exercise you are playing.

3) If you have a physical copy of the book, simply pencil in 16th notes over the top of the melody and then write in an accent over every 2+3 16th notes.

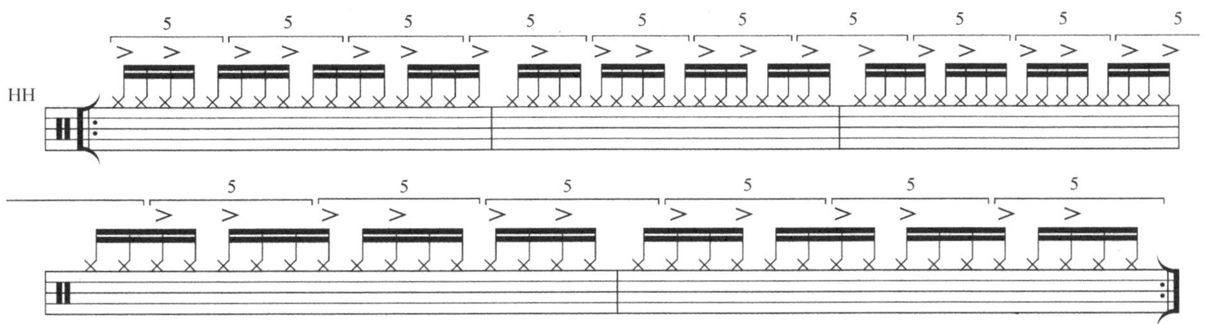

**Asterisks designate the measures where the accented groupings & phrases of "5" will reset on beat 1 again*

Exercise 24: Incorporating Displaced Moving Melody With the Ostinato

16th note rate grooves with groupings of 7 (7/16)

Below, you will find a transcription of the ostinato containing groupings of "7." However, this time, only the HH is included. Since the assignment utilizes movement of both bass drum & snare drum, the only constant pattern are the accents in the HH hand. The rest of the page contains the entire rhythmic melody that will be altered by assigning the bass drum & snare drum on the proper counts. There are 3 ways you can go about working on these exercise pages for independence & variation development:

1) On a separate piece of paper, write out the ostinato several times. Insert the assigned bass drum & snare drum notes from the melody below into the ostinato phrases you've transcribed.

2) Play down the whole exercise/melody and insert the accents (by ear) over the top of the exercise you are playing.

3) If you have a physical copy of the book, simply pencil in 16th notes over the top of the melody and then write in an accents over the 16th notes in 2+2+3 groupings.

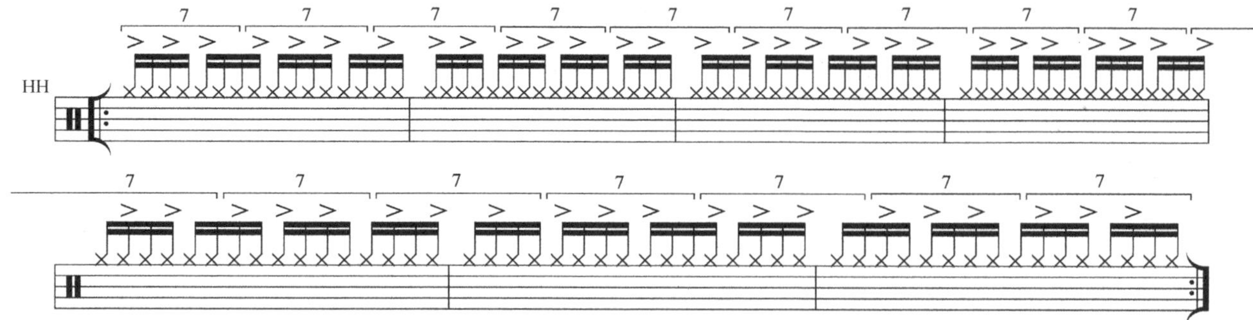

**Asterisks designate the measures where the accented groupings & phrases of "7" will reset on beat 1 again*

PART 3 CHANGE OF RATES

Polymetric Grooves with Various Tuplet Rates

Section 1 : TUPLETS

Groupings of “2” (or 2/8) over a triplet rate in 4/4

In this portion of the book, the meter will still remain in 4/4. However, this sub-chapter starts moving in an area that has not been examined up to this point. This section of the book will start to delve into the topic of ‘tuplets’ in which the standard rate subdivision of each quarter note (of 2, 4, 8, etc.…) expand into alternate choices (3, 5, 7, etc.…).

In a normal 4/4 meter comprising of consistent 8th note triplets on the HH, it’s safe to assume that one would eventually incorporate accents on downbeats to enhance the feel, sound and presence of the groove. The majority of drummers & instructors utilize and/or teach the usage of the Moeller technique to accurately execute the correct application of the accents. The breakdown of that HH pattern alone would look like this:

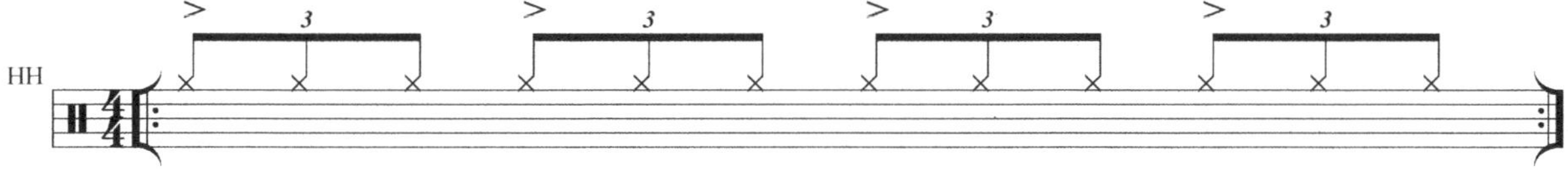

Adding the BD and SD in their proper places to create a “standard groove” with the triplet rate, the complete pattern is the very recognizable one seen here:

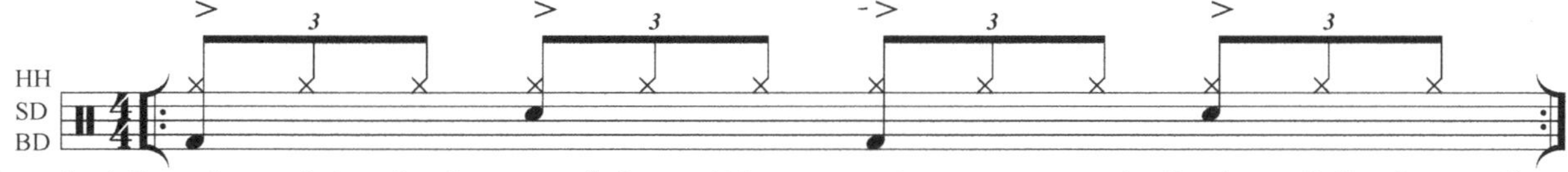

Notice that the above “standard groove” doesn’t incorporate any cross rhythmic activity due to the accents laying in groupings of “3” and being in sync with the BD & SD pattern. However, in order to start displacing the accents and creating cross rhythmic ideas in a groove setting, a good place to start is to incorporate other numbered groupings in the time hand or limbs. Below is the breakdown of the same HH pattern but now utilizing groupings of “2” to create a cross rhythmic pattern. Take note that, unlike previous sections, the groupings of 2 within a triplet rate don’t create an “over the bar” rhythm but it does allow for an illusive cross rhythmic feel.

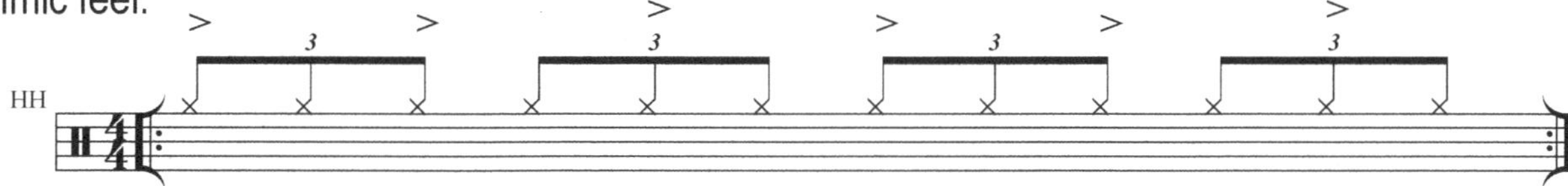

Tip Counting Exercise

A good suggested exercise for any cross rhythm is to count out loud even before playing as to help build the two existing rhythms internally. Below, you will find a single measure phrase consisting of only 8th note triplet note counts, but every 2nd symbol is in bold as to represent the placement of an accent. Start by counting out loud, accentuating the bolded symbols while tapping your foot on downbeats in 4/4:

| **1** trip **let** 2 **trip** let **3** trip **let** 4 **trip** let |

Primary Ostinato

The following pattern you see is the primary hand ostinato which will remain constant through the various grooves & exercises in this section. As your starting point, practice just this hand pattern together to develop independence involved in keeping the accents in groupings of "2" consistent over the top of the snare drum which remains on 2 & 4 throughout.

Practice Note: To obtain the most successful sound & feel of this ostinato, make sure that you are incorporating a repetitive 2-stroke Moeller accent technique in your time hand while you retain a consistent backbeat technique in the snare hand. Make an effort to ensure that the shifting accents do not affect or change the motion in either hand.

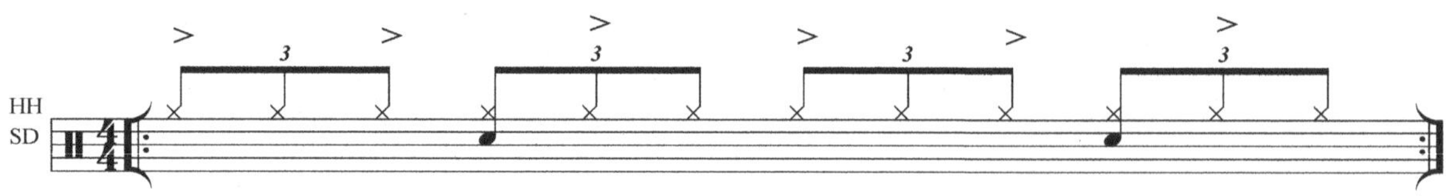

Incorporating the Bass Drum

The final goal is to now complete your phrases & grooves by adding countless bass drum rhythms to the ostinato. A great place to begin is to utilize any beginner drum set book with easy single-measure grooves. You can use any book that incorporates a triplet-based rate in the groove as your primary rate, or you can even use any 8th note rate grooves by swinging the 8th notes to create a triplet-based feel. Below is the basic groove followed by the same groove with the accents in groupings of "2" over the top in your time hand.

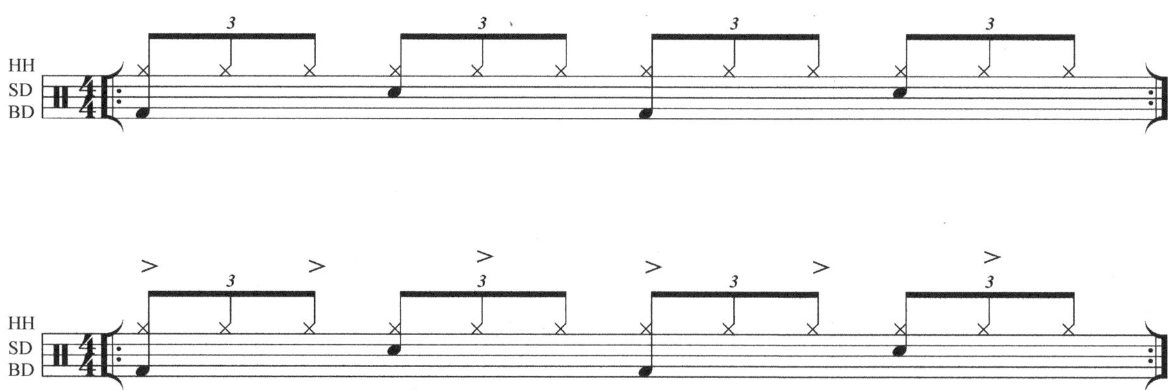

Exercise 25 : Basic Beats

8th note triplet rate grooves with groupings of 2 (2/8)

Below, you will find the transcription of the current ostinato once again. The rest of the page contains variations of simple grooves for bass drum variations. There are 3 ways you can go about working on these exercise pages for independence & variation development:

1) On a separate piece of paper, write out the ostinato 12 times. Extract the bass drum notes from the 12 single-measure grooves below and insert them into the ostinato phrases you've transcribed.

2) Play the single-measure phrases as many times as you would like, and insert the accents (by ear) over the top of the grooves you are playing.

3) If you have a physical copy of the book, simply pencil in a bass drum pattern from a single-measure phrase into the ostinato. Once comfortable, erase and then move to transcribing the next patterns down the page one-by-one.

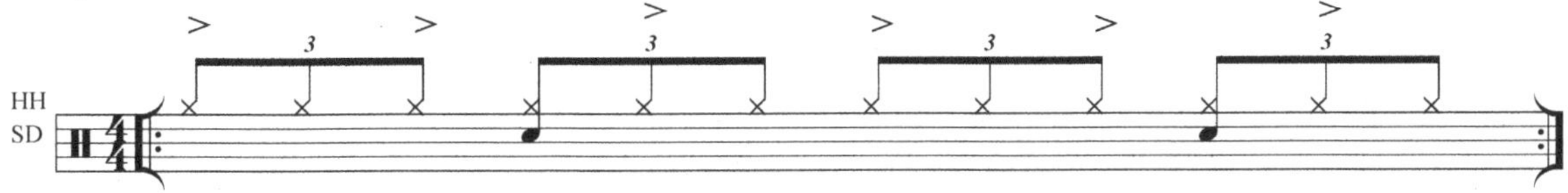

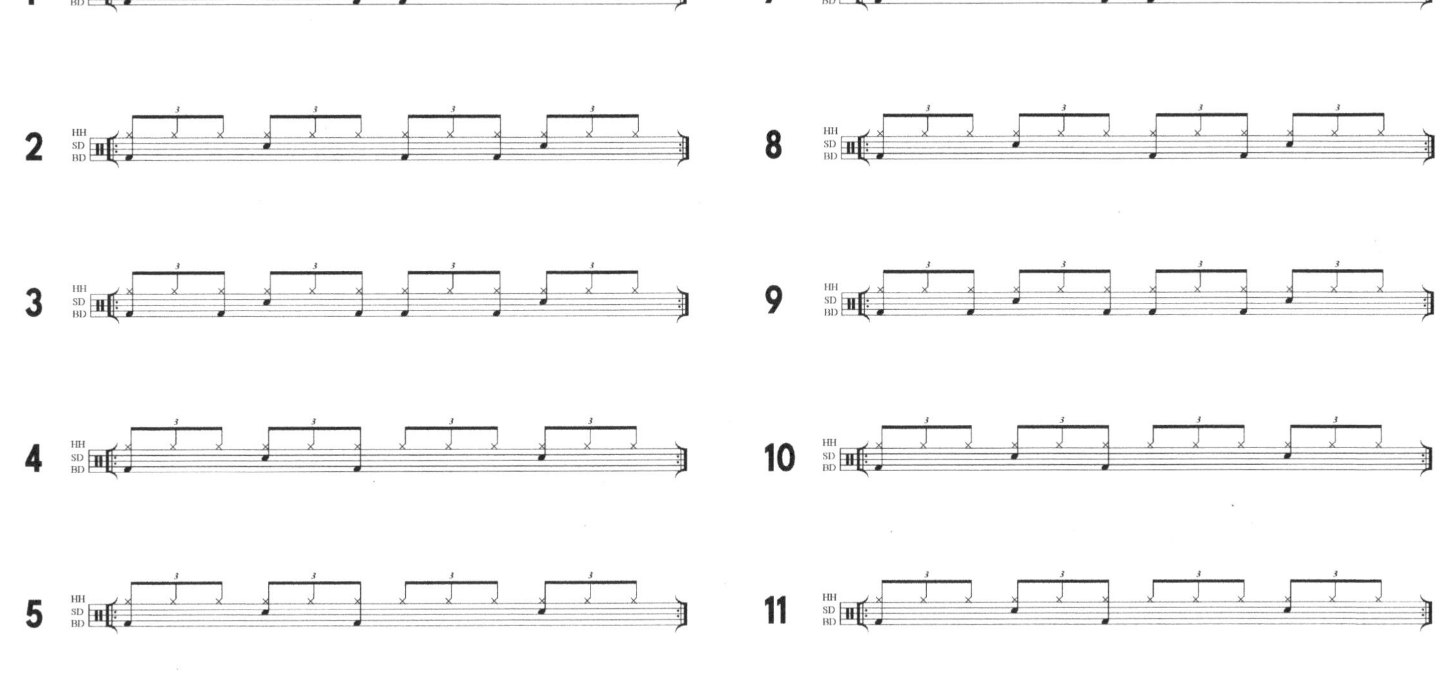

Incorporating a Syncopated Bass Drum Moving Melody

Quarter Note, 8th Note and Triplet Partials

The next step in varying your bass drum would be to combine an individual syncopated ongoing melody with the current 8th note triplet ostinato. The melody you will see in the next section is written as if were a snare melody, but you have the option of applying it to any limb that is applied to the kit. For the current exercises, we will be applying it to or playing it on the bass drum. The most appropriate book to use in this current rhythmic category is *Syncopation for the Modern Drummer* by Ted Reed. The full melody is an example of a page you will find in that book.

Below, find the example of line 1 of the syncopated exercise (found on the next page) and how it is then applied to the bass drum under the current ostinato with groupings of "2." Take note that the melody comprises of various partials of 8th note triplet groupings: quarter notes (falling on beat 1 of every triplet grouping), a middle triplet note, and then notes that fall on the "+" of each measure (which occur on the last note of every triplet grouping). Here is an illustration of the combination process, putting the hand pattern and the bass drum melody together. ****NOTE***: Keep in mind this is a similar syncopated melody used in previous pages, but it now incorporates notes that fall on the middle note of a triplet grouping.

Primary Ostinato

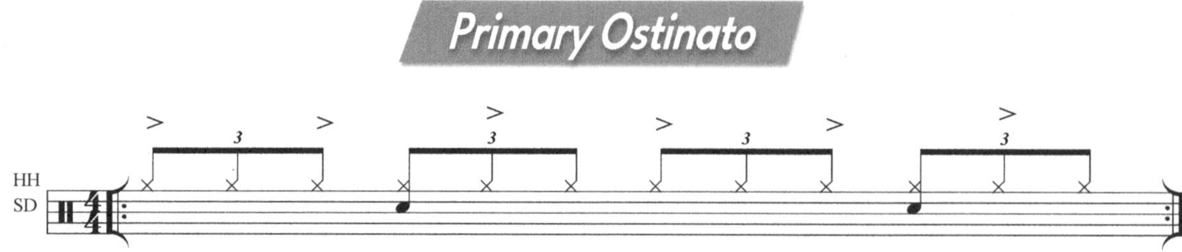

Bass Drum Melody (first 4 measures)

Combination (full phrase)

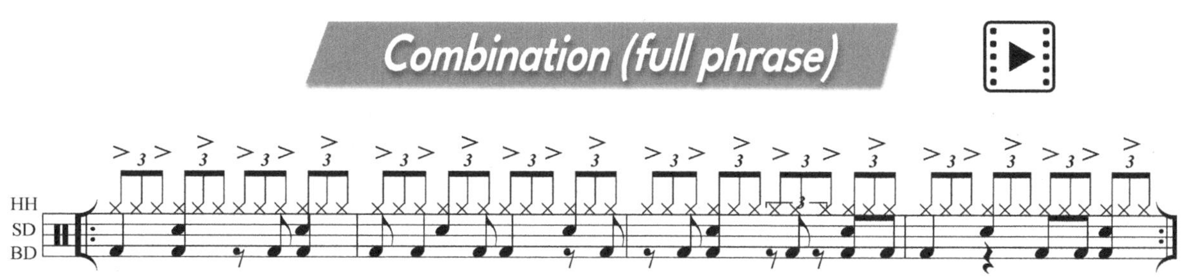

Exercise 26 : Syncopated Moving Melody with Quarter Note, 8th Note and Triplet Partials

8th note triplet rate grooves with groupings of 2 (2/8)

Below, you will find the transcription of the current ostinato once again. The rest of the page contains the entire rhythmic melody that will be applied to the bass drum. There are 3 ways you can go about working on these exercise pages for independence & variation development:

1) On a separate piece of paper, write out the ostinato 24 times. Insert the bass drum notes from the melody below into the ostinato phrases you've transcribed.

2) Play down the whole exercise/melody and insert the accents (by ear) over the top of the exercise you are playing.

3) If you have a physical copy of the book, simply pencil in 8th note triplets over the top of the melody and then write in an accent over every 2nd 8th note.

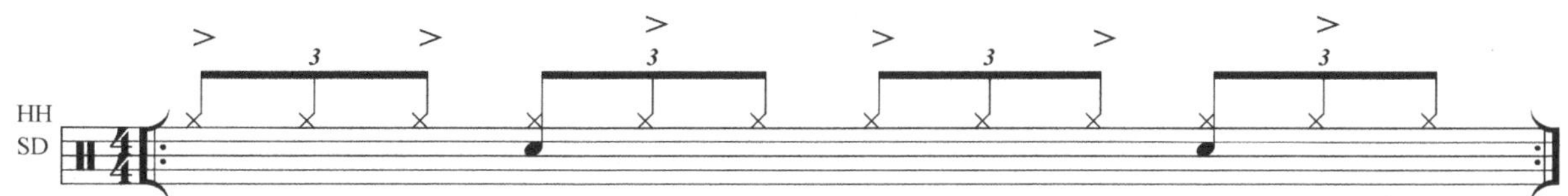

No asterisks are needed to mark off odd-measure phrases as the ostinato resets after every bar in this current exercise

Section 2 : TUPLETS

Groupings of "4" (or 4/8) over a triplet rate in 4/4

Continuing the topic of 'tuplets' in which the standard rate subdivision of each quarter note (of 2, 4, 8, etc....) expand into alternate choices (3, 5, 7, etc....), the triplet will remain the consistent rate for this section once again. This time, however, the accents in our cross rhythm feel will change.

In a normal 4/4 meter comprising of consistent 8th note *triplets* on the HH, it's safe to assume that one would eventually incorporate accents on downbeats to enhance the feel, sound and presence of the groove. The majority of drummers & instructors utilize and/or teach the usage of the Moeller technique to accurately execute the correct application of the accents. The breakdown of that HH pattern alone would look like this:

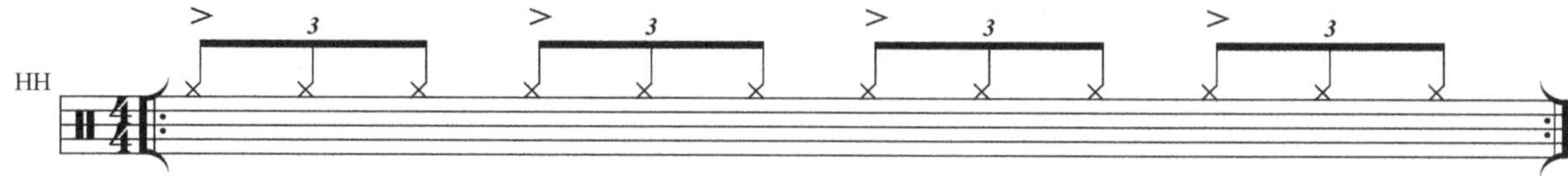

Adding the BD and SD in their proper places to create a "standard groove" with the triplet rate, the complete pattern is the very recognizable one seen here:

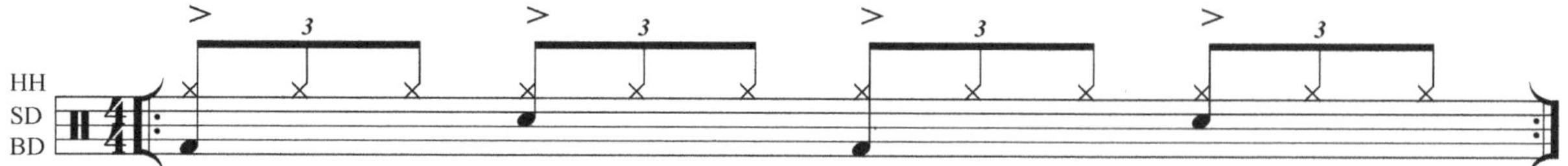

Notice that the above "standard groove" doesn't incorporate any cross rhythmic activity due to the accents laying in groupings of "3" and being in sync with the BD & SD pattern. However, in order to start displacing the accents and creating cross rhythmic ideas in a groove setting, a good place to start is to incorporate other numbered groupings in the time hand or limbs. Below is the breakdown of the same HH pattern but now utilizing groupings of "4" to create a cross rhythmic pattern. Take note that, like previous triplet section, the groupings of 4 within a triplet rate don't create an "over the bar" rhythm but it does allow for an illusive cross rhythmic feel.

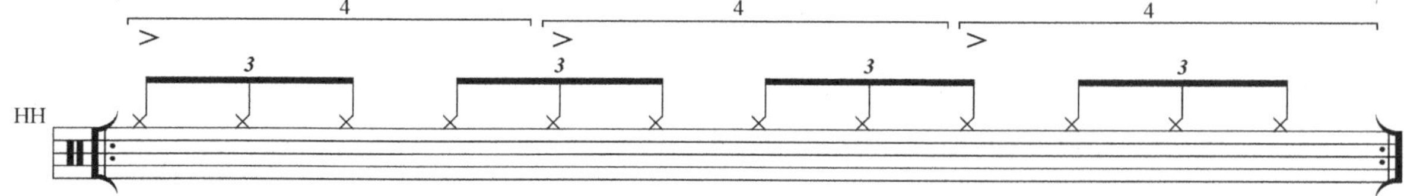

Tip: Counting Exercise

A good suggested exercise for any cross rhythm is to count out loud even before playing as to help build the two existing rhythms internally. Below, you will find a single measure phrase consisting of only 8th note triplet note counts, but every 4th symbol is in bold as to represent the placement of an accent. Start by counting out loud, accentuating the bolded symbols while tapping your foot on downbeats in 4/4:

| **1** trip let 2 **trip** let 3 trip **let** 4 trip let |

Primary Ostinato

The following pattern you see is the primary hand ostinato which will remain constant through the various grooves & exercises in this section. As your starting point, practice just this hand pattern together to develop independence involved in keeping the accents in groupings of "4" consistent over the top of the snare drum which remains on 2 & 4 throughout.

Practice Note: To obtain the most successful sound & feel of this ostinato, make sure that you are incorporating a repetitive 4-stroke Moeller accent technique in your time hand while you retain a consistent backbeat technique in the snare hand. Make an effort to ensure that the shifting accents do not affect or change the motion in either hand.

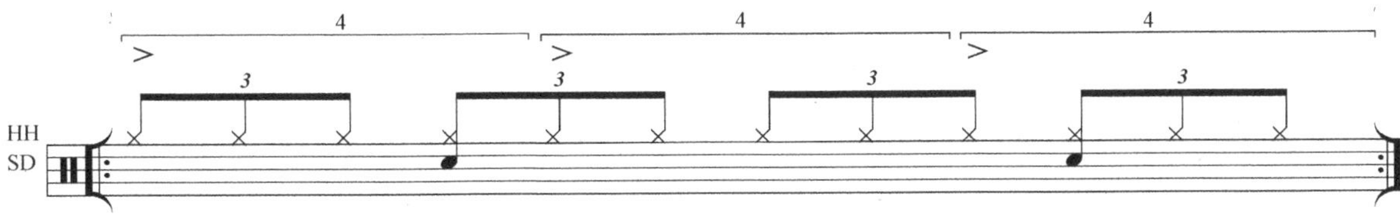

Incorporating the Bass Drum

The final goal is to now complete your phrases & grooves by adding countless bass drum rhythms to the ostinato. A great place to begin is to utilize any beginner drum set book with easy single-measure grooves. You can use any book that incorporates a triplet-based rate in the groove as your primary rate, or you can even use any 8th note rate grooves by swinging the 8th notes to create a triplet-based feel. Below is the basic groove followed by the same groove with the accents in groupings of "4" over the top in your time hand.

Exercise 27: Basic Beats

8th note triplet rate grooves with groupings of 4 (4/8)

Below, you will find the transcription of the current ostinato once again. The rest of the page contains variations of simple grooves for bass drum variations. There are 3 ways you can go about working on these exercise pages for independence & variation development:

1) On a separate piece of paper, write out the ostinato 12 times. Extract the bass drum notes from the 12 single-measure grooves below and insert them into the ostinato phrases you've transcribed.

2) Play the single-measure phrases as many times as you would like, and insert the accents (by ear) over the top of the grooves you are playing.

3) f you have a physical copy of the book, simply pencil in a bass drum pattern from a single-measure phrase into the ostinato. Once comfortable, erase and then move to transcribing the next patterns down the page one-by-one.

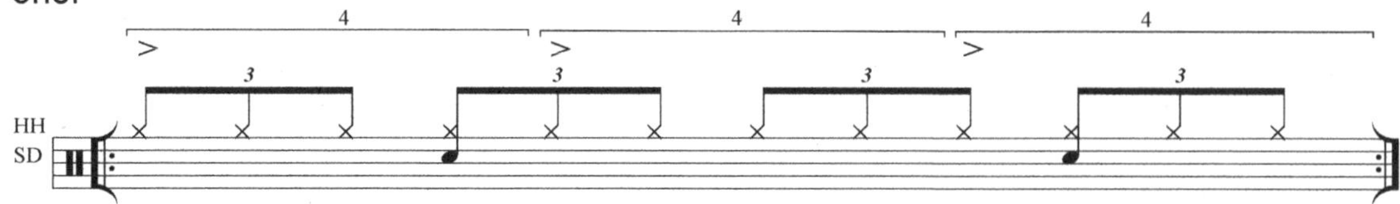

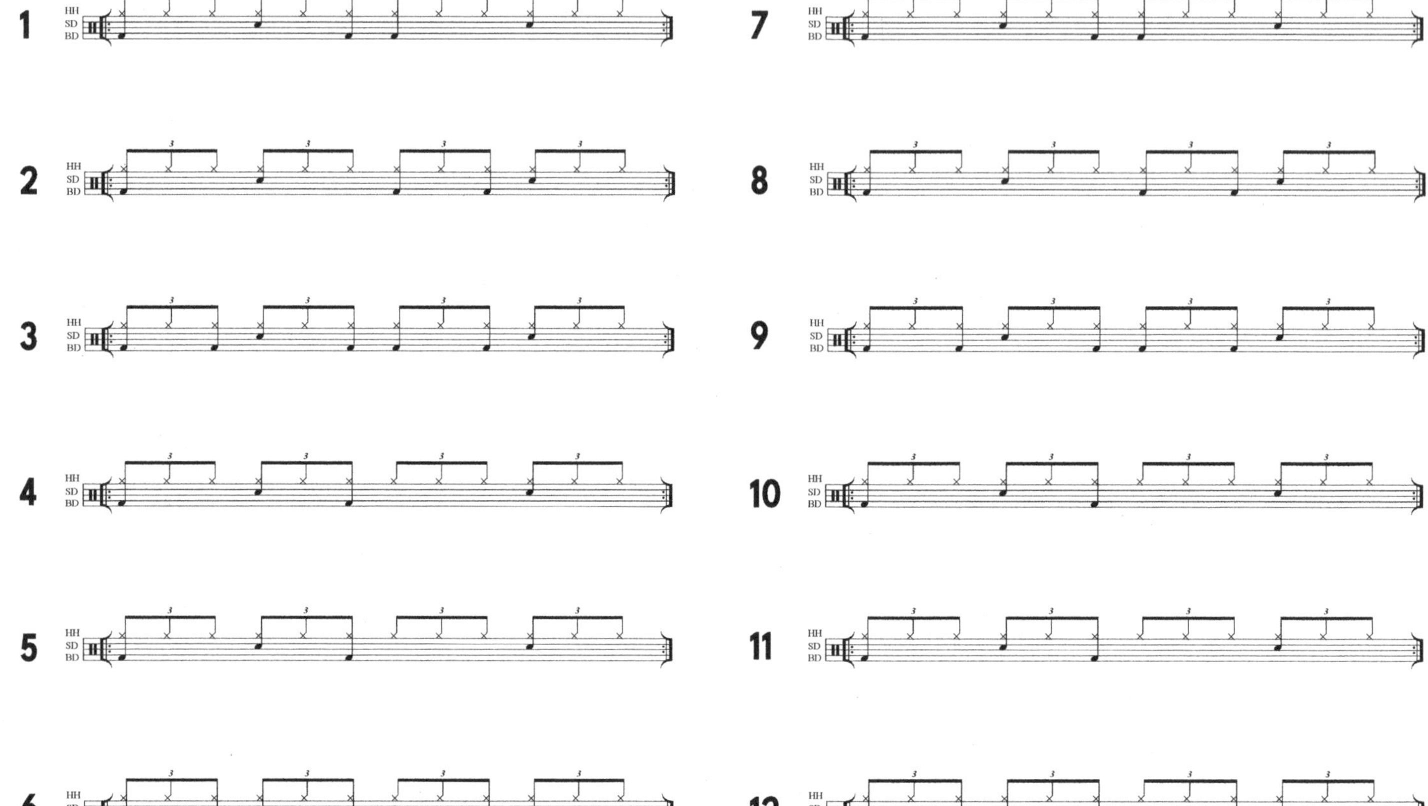

Incorporating a Syncopated Bass Drum Moving Melody

Quarter Note, 8th Note and Triplet Partials

The next step in varying your bass drum would be to combine an individual syncopated ongoing melody with the current 8th note triplet ostinato. The melody you will see in the next section is written as if were a snare melody, but you have the option of applying it to any limb that is applied to the kit. For the current exercises, we will be applying it to or playing it on the bass drum. The most appropriate book to use in this current rhythmic category is *Syncopation for the Modern Drummer* by Ted Reed. The full melody is an example of a page you will find in that book.

Below, find the example of line 1 of the syncopated exercise (found on the next page) and how it is then applied to the bass drum under the current ostinato with groupings of "4." Take note that the melody comprises of various partials of 8th note triplet groupings: quarter notes (falling on beat 1 of every triplet grouping), a middle triplet note, and then notes that fall on the "+" of each measure (which occur on the last note of every triplet grouping). Here is an illustration of the combination process, putting the hand pattern and the bass drum melody together. ***NOTE:*** Keep in mind this is a similar syncopated melody used in previous pages, but it now incorporates notes that fall on the middle note of a triplet grouping.

Primary Ostinato

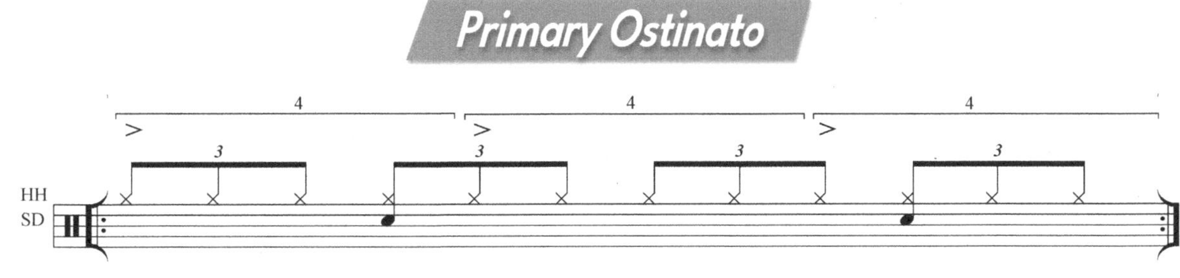

Bass Drum Melody (first 4 measures)

Combination (full phrase)

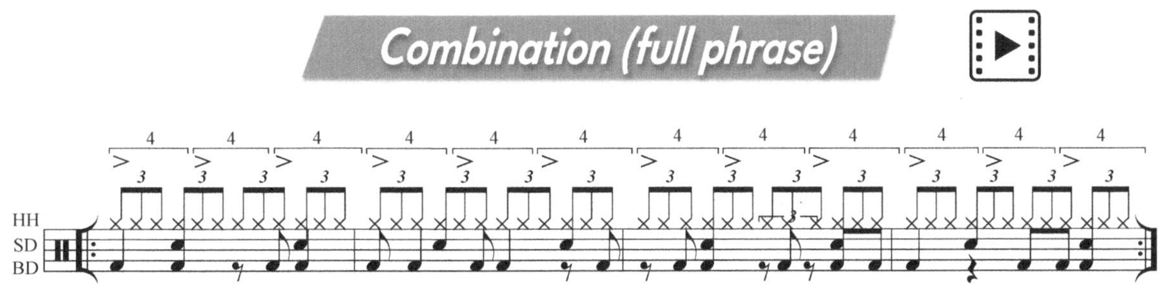

Exercise 28 : Syncopated Moving Melody with Quarter Note, 8th Note and Triplet Partials

8th note triplet rate grooves with groupings of 4 (4/8)

Below, you will find the transcription of the current ostinato once again. The rest of the page contains the entire rhythmic melody that will be applied to the bass drum. There are 3 ways you can go about working on these exercise pages for independence & variation development:

1) On a separate piece of paper, write out the ostinato 24 times. Insert the bass drum notes from the melody below into the ostinato phrases you've transcribed.

2) Play down the whole exercise/melody and insert the accents (by ear) over the top of the exercise you are playing.

3) If you have a physical copy of the book, simply pencil in 8th note triplets over the top of the melody and then write in an accent over every 4th 8th note.

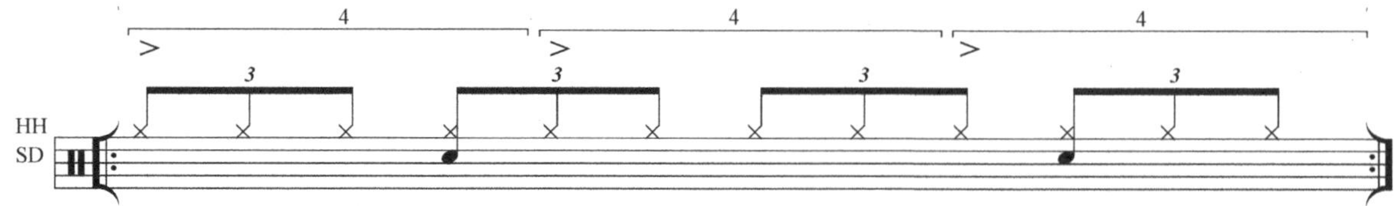

No asterisks are needed to mark off odd-measure phrases as the ostinato resets after every bar in this current exercise

Section 3 : TUPLETS

Groupings of “5” (or 5/8) over a triplet rate in 4/4

Continuing the topic of ‘tuplets’ in which the standard rate subdivision of each quarter note (of 2, 4, 8, etc.…) expand into alternate choices (3, 5, 7, etc.…), the triplet will remain the consistent rate for this section once again. The accents in our cross rhythm feel will now change to a grouping much more complicated.

In a normal 4/4 meter comprising of consistent 8th note *triplets* on the HH, it’s safe to assume that one would eventually incorporate accents on downbeats to enhance the feel, sound and presence of the groove. The majority of drummers & instructors utilize and/or teach the usage of the Moeller technique to accurately execute the correct application of the accents. The breakdown of that HH pattern alone would look like this:

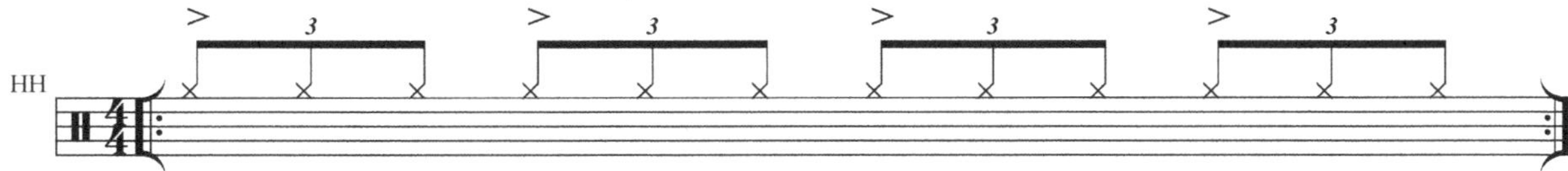

Adding the BD and SD in their proper places to create a “standard groove” with the triplet rate, the complete pattern is the very recognizable one seen here:

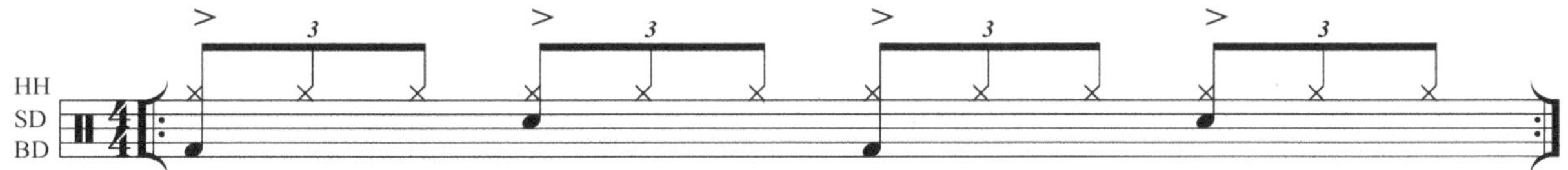

Notice that the above “standard groove” doesn’t incorporate any cross rhythmic activity due to the accents laying in groupings of “3” and being in sync with the BD & SD pattern. However, in order to start displacing the accents and creating cross rhythmic ideas in a groove setting, a good place to start is to incorporate other numbered groupings in the time hand or limbs. Below is the breakdown of the same HH pattern but now utilizing groupings of “5” to create a cross rhythmic pattern. Now, the “over the bar” cross rhythm is present as it takes 5 bars to come back around to beat 1. For practicality & musical purposes, the phrases you see will be organized with a 2+3 phrasing.

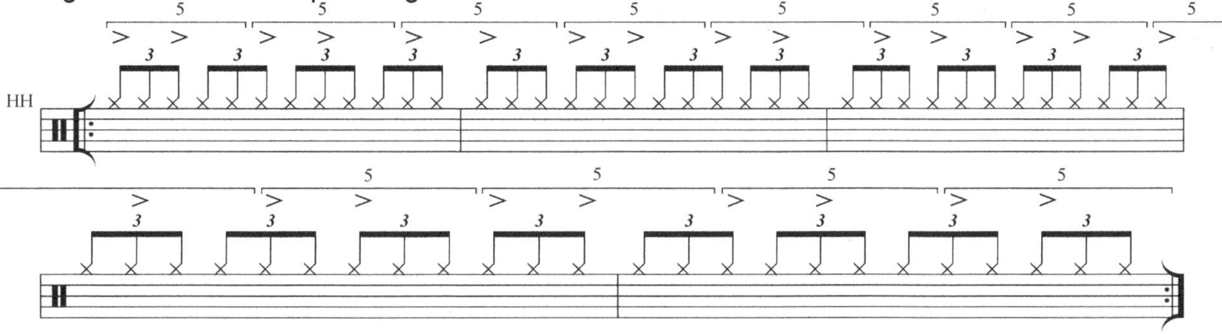

Tip: Counting Exercise

A good suggested exercise for any cross rhythm is to count out loud even before playing as to help build the two existing rhythms internally. Below, you will find a single measure phrase consisting of only 8th note triplet note counts, but every 4th symbol is in bold as to represent the placement of an accent. Start by counting out loud, accentuating the bolded symbols while tapping your foot on downbeats in 4/4:

| **1** trip **let** 2 trip **let** 3 **trip** let 4 **trip** let | **1** trip let **2** trip **let** 3 trip **let** 4 **trip** let | 1 **trip** let **2** trip let **3** trip **let** 4 trip **let** |

| 1 **trip** let 2 **trip** let **3** trip let **4** trip **let** | 1 trip **let** 2 **trip** let 3 **trip** let **4** trip let |

Primary Ostinato

The following pattern you see is the primary hand ostinato which will remain constant through the various grooves & exercises in this section. As your starting point, practice just this hand pattern together to develop independence involved in keeping the accents, this time, in groupings of "5," consistent over the top of the snare drum which remains on beats 2 & 4 throughout. Remember that the subdivision break up for your groupings of "5" is a 2+3 phrase.

Practice Note: To obtain the most successful sound & feel of this ostinato, make sure that you are incorporating a repetitive Moeller accent technique in 2 strokes, then 3 strokes, each phrase in your time hand while you retain a consistent backbeat technique in the snare hand. Make an effort to ensure that the shifting accents do not affect or change the motion in either hand.

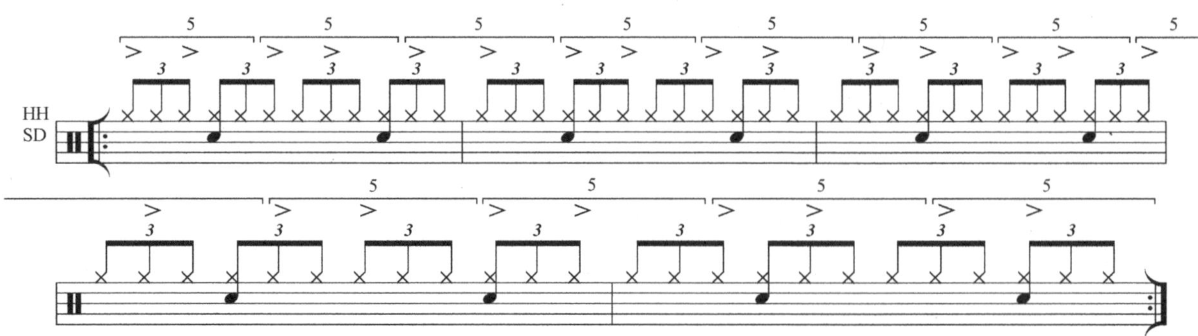

Incorporating the Bass Drum

The final goal is to now complete your phrases & grooves by adding countless bass drum rhythms to the ostinato. A great place to begin is to utilize any beginner drum set book with easy single-measure grooves. You can use any book that incorporates a triplet-based rate in the groove as your primary rate, or you can even use any 8th note rate grooves by swinging the 8th notes to create a triplet-based feel. Below is the basic groove followed by the same groove with the accents in groupings of "5" (2+3) over the top in your time hand.

Exercise 29: Basic Beats

8th note triplet rate grooves with groupings of 5 (5/8)

Below, you will find the transcription of the current ostinato once again. The rest of the page contains variations of simple grooves for bass drum variations. There are 3 ways you can go about working on these exercise pages for independence & variation development:

1) On a separate piece of paper, write out the ostinato 12 times. Extract the bass drum notes from the 12 single-measure grooves below and insert them into the ostinato phrases you've transcribed.

2) Play the single-measure phrases 5 times each,and insert the accents (by ear) over the top of the grooves you are playing.

3) f you have a physical copy of the book, simply pencil in a bass drum pattern from a single-measure phrase into the ostinato. Once comfortable, erase and then move to transcribing the next patterns down the page one-by-one.

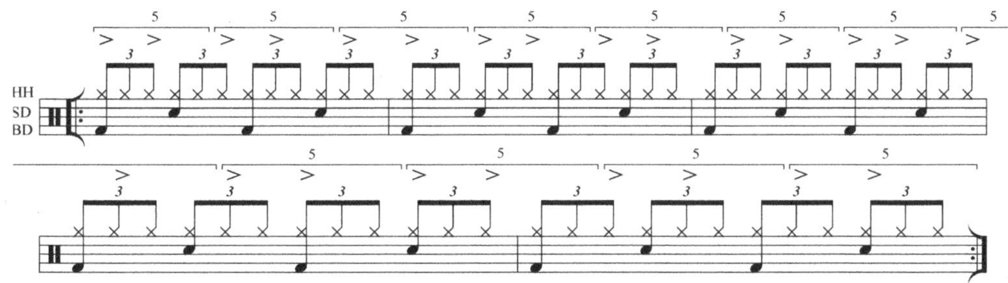

1 

7 

2 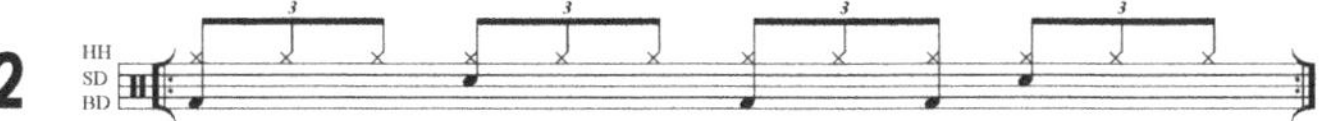

8 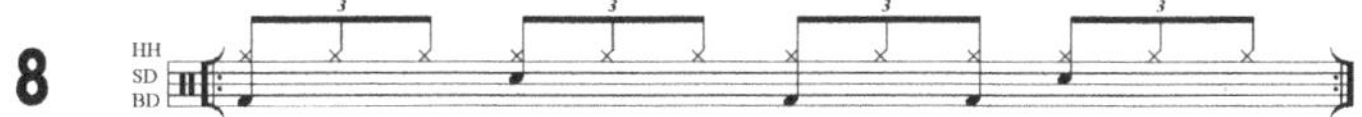

3 

9 

4 

10 

5 

11 

6 

12 

Incorporating a Syncopated Bass Drum Moving Melody

Quarter Note, 8th Note and Triplet Partials

The next step in varying your bass drum would be to combine an individual syncopated ongoing melody with the current 8th note triplet ostinato. The melody you will see in the next section is written as if were a snare melody, but you have the option of applying it to any limb that is applied to the kit. For the current exercises, we will be applying it to or playing it on the bass drum. The most appropriate book to use in this current rhythmic category is *Syncopation for the Modern Drummer* by Ted Reed. The full melody is an example of a page you will find in that book.

Below, find the example of the first 5 measures of the syncopated exercise (found on the next page) and how it is then applied to the bass drum under the current ostinato with groupings of "5" (2+3 grouping). Take note that the melody comprises of various partials of 8th note triplet groupings: quarter notes (falling on beat 1 of every triplet grouping), a middle triplet note, and then notes that fall on the "+" of each measure (which occur on the last note of every triplet grouping). Here is an illustration of the combination process, putting the hand pattern and the bass drum melody together. ***NOTE:*** Keep in mind this is a similar syncopated melody used in previous pages, but it now incorporates notes that fall on the middle note of a triplet grouping.

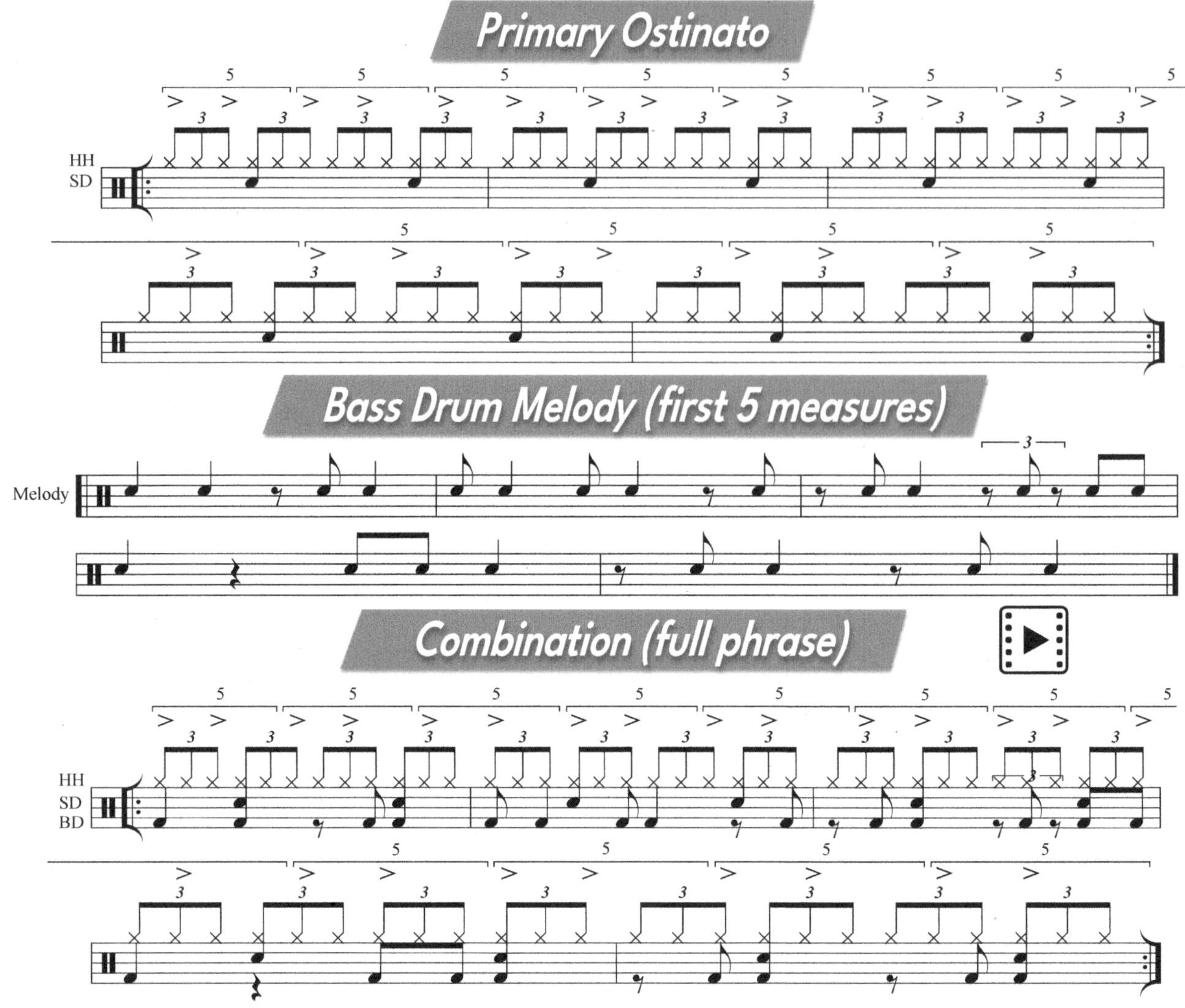

Exercise 30: Syncopated Moving Melody with Quarter Note, 8th Note and Triplet Partials

8th note triplet rate grooves with groupings of 5 (5/8)

Below, you will find the transcription of the current ostinato once again. The rest of the page contains the entire rhythmic melody that will be applied to the bass drum. There are 3 ways you can go about working on these exercise pages for independence & variation development:

1) On a separate piece of paper, write out the ostinato several times. Insert the bass drum notes from the melody below into the ostinato phrases you've transcribed.

2) Play down the whole exercise/melody and insert the accents (by ear) over the top of the exercise you are playing.

3) If you have a physical copy of the book, simply pencil in 8th note triplets over the top of the melody and then write in 2+3 groupings over the ongoing 8th note triplets.

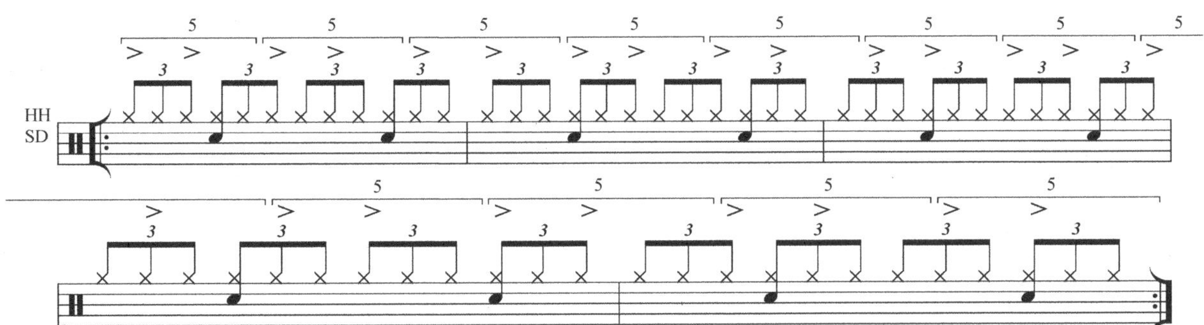

** Asterisks designate the measures where the accented groupings & phrases of "5" will reset on beat 1 again*

Section 4 : TUPLETS

Groupings of "7" (or 7/8) over a triplet rate in 4/4

Continuing the topic of 'tuplets' in which the standard rate subdivision of each quarter note (of 2, 4, 8, etc.…) expand into alternate choices (3, 5, 7, etc.…), the triplet will remain the consistent rate for this section once again. The accents in our cross rhythm feel will now change to a grouping much more complicated.

In a normal 4/4 meter comprising of consistent 8th note *triplets* on the HH, it's safe to assume that one would eventually incorporate accents on downbeats to enhance the feel, sound and presence of the groove. The majority of drummers & instructors utilize and/or teach the usage of the Moeller technique to accurately execute the correct application of the accents. The breakdown of that HH pattern alone would look like this:

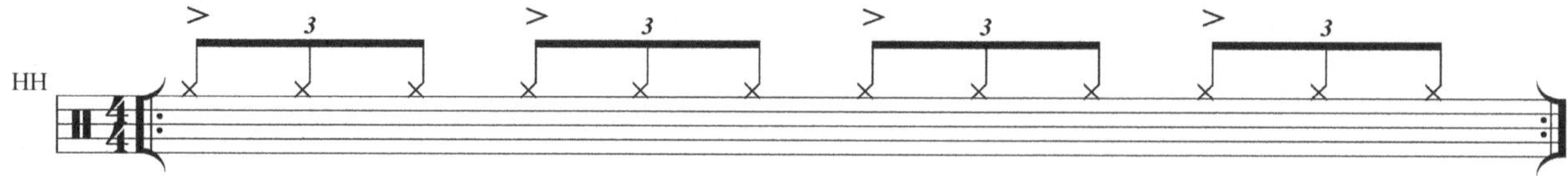

Adding the BD and SD in their proper places to create a "standard groove" with the triplet rate, the complete pattern is the very recognizable one seen here:

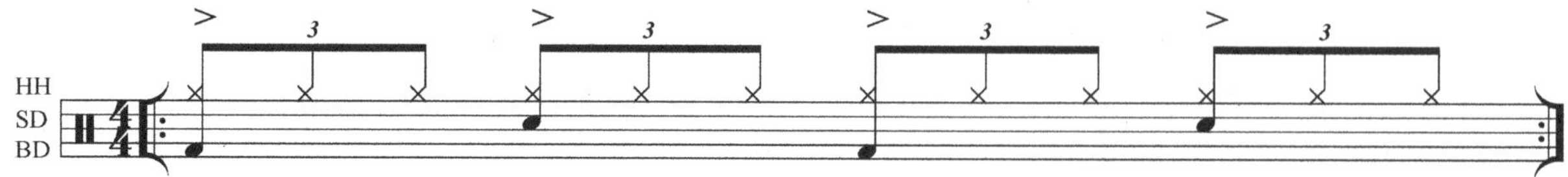

Notice that the above "standard groove" doesn't incorporate any cross rhythmic activity due to the accents laying in groupings of "3" and being in sync with the BD & SD pattern. However, in order to start displacing the accents and creating cross rhythmic ideas in a groove setting, a good place to start is to incorporate other numbered groupings in the time hand or limbs. Below is the breakdown of the same HH pattern but now utilizing groupings of "7" to create a cross rhythmic pattern. Now, the "over the bar" cross rhythm is present as it takes 7 bars to come back around to beat 1. For practicality & musical purposes, the phrases you see will be organized with a 2+2+3 phrasing.

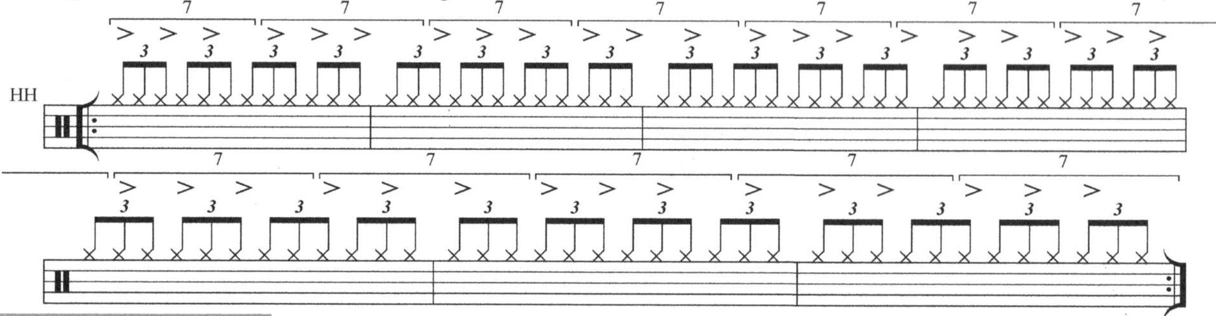

Tip: Counting Exercise

A good suggested exercise for any cross rhythm is to count out loud even before playing as to help build the two existing rhythms internally. Below, you will find a 7 measure phrase consisting of only 8th note triplet note counts, but every symbol in bold is representing the placement of an accent in a 2+2+3 subdivided phrase. Start by counting out loud, accentuating the bolded symbols while tapping your foot on downbeats in 4/4:

| **1** trip **let** 2 **trip** let 3 **trip** let **4** trip **let** | 1 trip **let** 2 **trip** let **3** trip let **4** trip **let** | 1 **trip** let 2 **trip** let **3** trip **let** 4 trip **let** |

| 1 **trip** let **2** trip let **3** trip **let** 4 **trip** let | 1 **trip** let **2** trip **let** 3 trip **let** 4 **trip** let | **1** trip let **2** trip **let** 3 **trip** let 4 **trip** let |

| **1** trip **let** 2 trip **let** 3 **trip** let **4** trip let |

Primary Ostinato

The following pattern you see is the primary hand ostinato which will remain constant through the various grooves & exercises in this section. As your starting point, practice just this hand pattern together to develop independence involved in keeping the accents, this time, in groupings of "7," consistent over the top of the snare drum which remains on beats 2 & 4 throughout. Remember that the subdivision break up for your groupings of "7" is a 2+2+3 phrase.

Practice Note: To obtain the most successful sound & feel of this ostinato, make sure that you are incorporating a repetitive Moeller accent technique in 2 strokes, then 2 strokes, then 3 strokes, each phrase in your time hand while you retain a consistent backbeat technique in the snare hand. Make an effort to ensure that the shifting accents do not affect or change the motion in either hand.

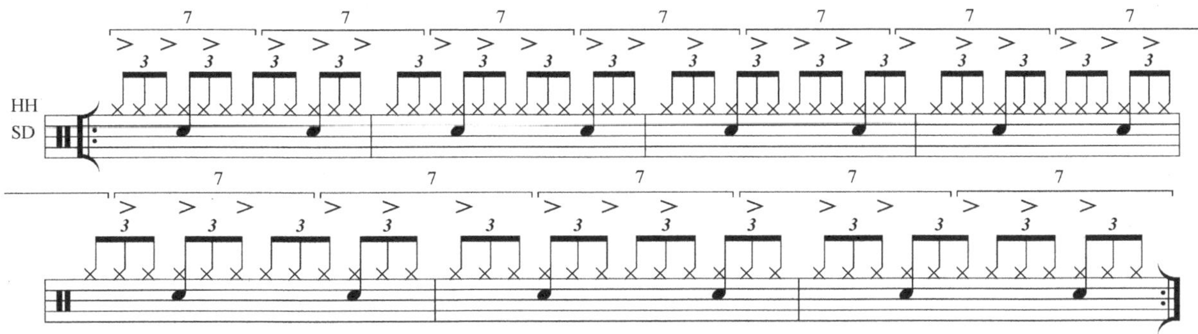

Incorporating the Bass Drum

The final goal is to now complete your phrases & grooves by adding countless bass drum rhythms to the ostinato. A great place to begin is to utilize any beginner drum set book with easy single-measure grooves. You can use any book that incorporates a triplet-based rate in the groove as your primary rate, or you can even use any 8th note rate grooves by swinging the 8th notes to create a triplet-based feel. Below is the basic groove followed by the same groove with the accents in groupings of "7" (2+2+3) over the top in your time hand.

Exercise 31: Basic Beats

8th note triplet rate grooves with groupings of 7 (7/8)

Below, you will find the transcription of the current ostinato once again. The rest of the page contains variations of simple grooves for bass drum variations. There are 3 ways you can go about working on these exercise pages for independence & variation development:

1) On a separate piece of paper, write out the ostinato 12 times. Extract the bass drum notes from the 12 single-measure grooves below and insert them into the ostinato phrases you've transcribed.

2) Play the single-measure phrases 7 times each, and insert the accents (by ear) over the top of the grooves you are playing.

3) If you have a physical copy of the book, simply pencil in a bass drum pattern from a single-measure phrase into the ostinato. Once comfortable, erase and then move to transcribing the next patterns down the page one-by-one.

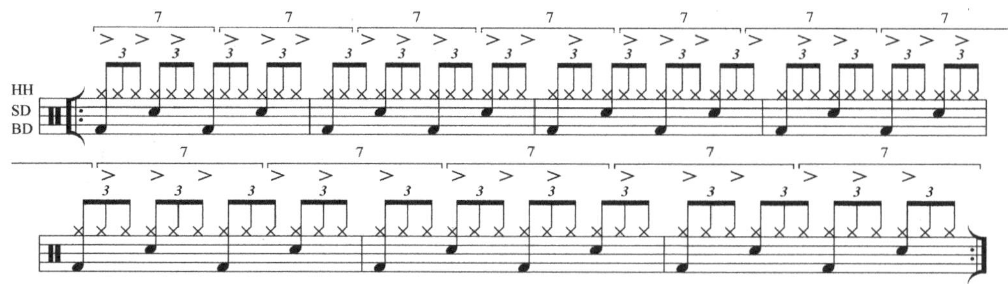

1 

7 

2 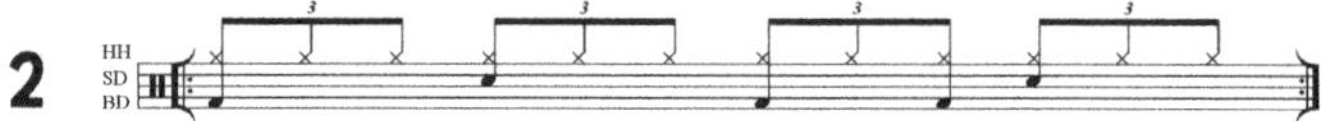

8 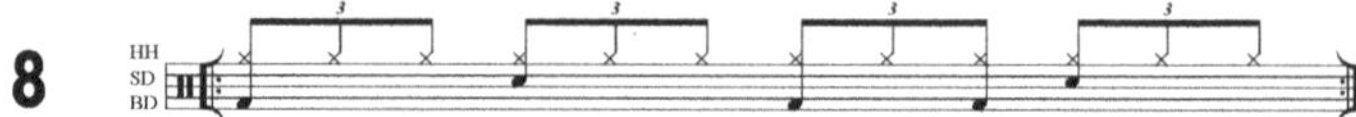

3 

9 

4 

10 

5 

11 

6 

12 

Incorporating a Syncopated Bass Drum Moving Melody

Quarter Note, 8th Note and Triplet Partials

The next step in varying your bass drum would be to combine an individual syncopated ongoing melody with the current 8th note triplet ostinato. The melody you will see in the next section is written as if were a snare melody, but you have the option of applying it to any limb that is applied to the kit. For the current exercises, we will be applying it to or playing it on the bass drum. The most appropriate book to use in this current rhythmic category is *Syncopation for the Modern Drummer* by Ted Reed. The full melody is an example of a page you will find in that book.

Below, find the example of the first 7 measures of the syncopated exercise (found on the next page) and how it is then applied to the bass drum under the current ostinato with groupings of "7" (2+2+3 grouping). Take note that the melody comprises of various partials of 8th note triplet groupings: quarter notes (falling on beat 1 of every triplet grouping), a middle triplet note, and then notes that fall on the "+" of each measure (which occur on the last note of every triplet grouping). Here is an illustration of the combination process, putting the hand pattern and the bass drum melody together. ***NOTE:*** Keep in mind this is a similar syncopated melody used in previous pages, but it now incorporates notes that fall on the middle note of a triplet grouping.

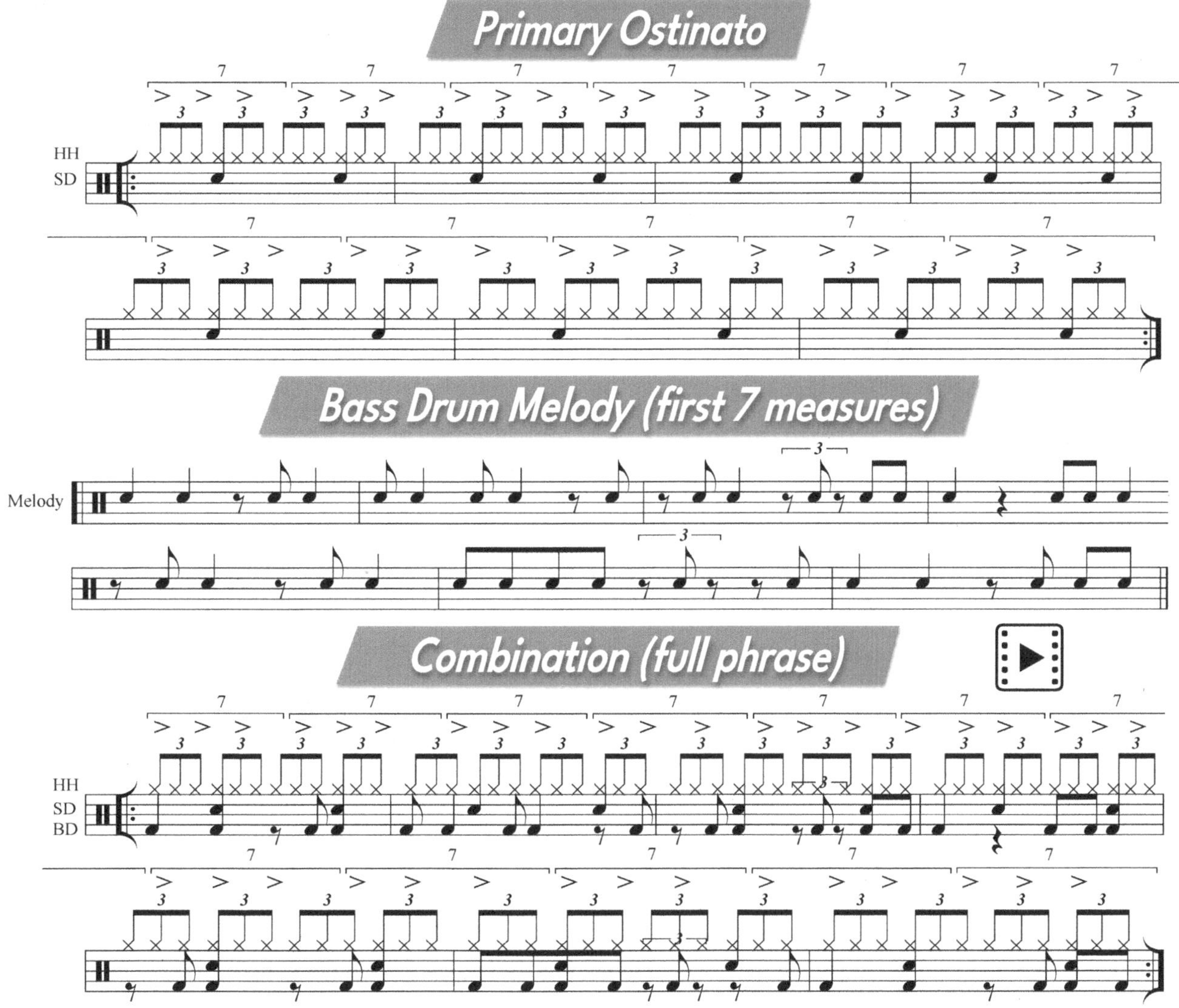

Exercise 32 : Syncopated Moving Melody with Quarter Note, 8th Note and Triplet Partials

8th note triplet rate grooves with groupings of 7 (7/8)

Below, you will find the transcription of the current ostinato once again. The rest of the page contains the entire rhythmic melody that will be applied to the bass drum. There are 3 ways you can go about working on these exercise pages for independence & variation development:

1) On a separate piece of paper, write out the ostinato several times. Insert the bass drum notes from the melody below into the ostinato phrases you've transcribed.

2) Play down the whole exercise/melody and insert the accents (by ear) over the top of the exercise you are playing.

3) If you have a physical copy of the book, simply pencil in 8th note triplets over the top of the melody and then write in 2+2+3 groupings over the ongoing 8th note triplets.

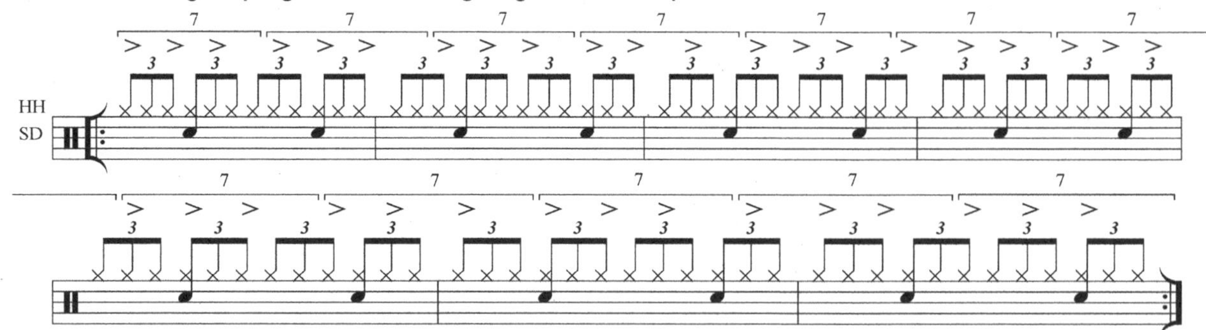

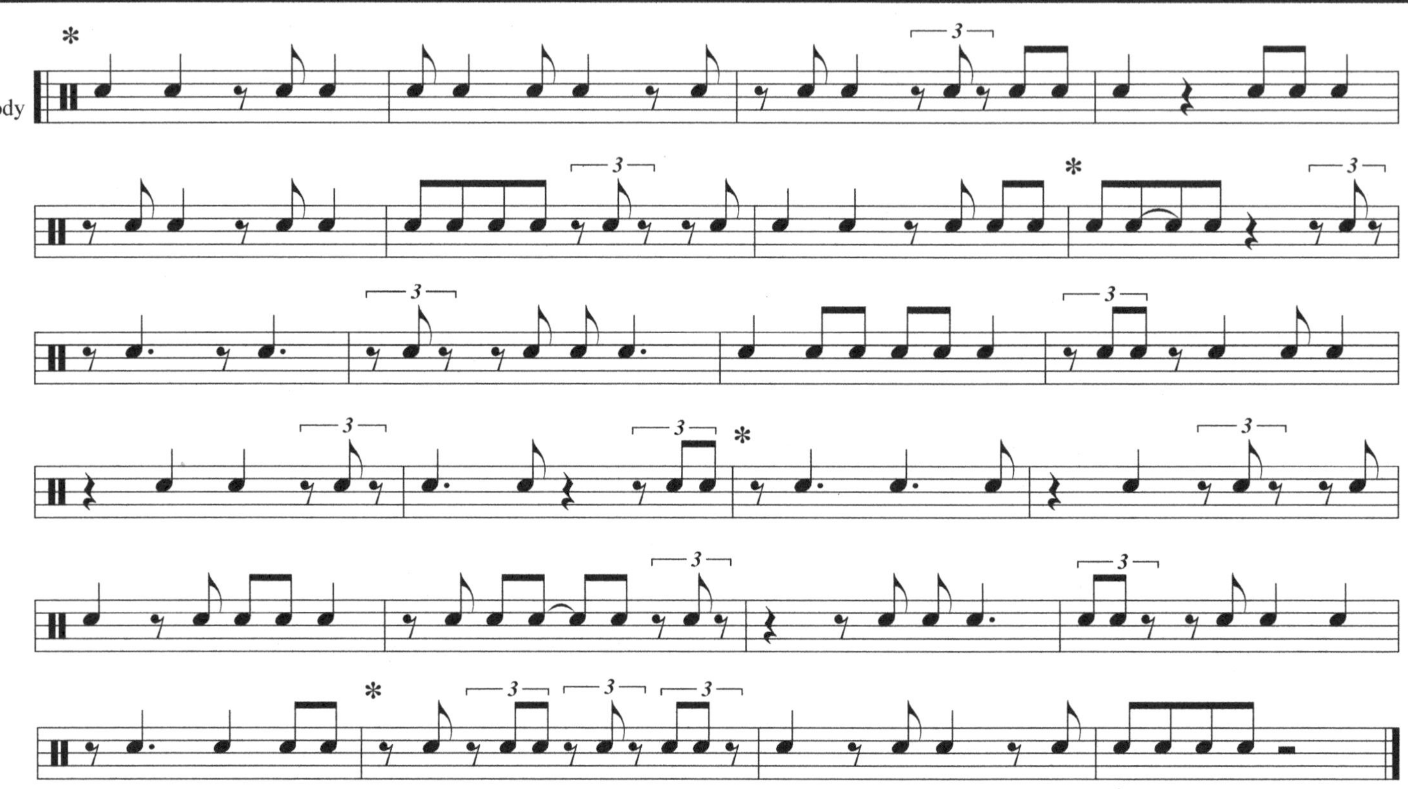

* *Asterisks designate the measures where the accented groupings & phrases of "7" will reset on beat 1 again*

Section 5 : TUPLETS

Groupings of "2" over a 16th note quintuplet rate in 4/4

In this portion of the book, the meter will still remain in 4/4. However, this next section starts moving into a more difficult area that has yet to be examined. Continuing the topic of 'tuplets' in which the standard rate subdivision of each quarter note (of 2, 4, 8, etc....) expands into alternate choices (3, 5, 7, etc....), this segment of the book introduces the topic of 16th note quintuplets, or groupings beamed in 5 notes.

In a normal 4/4 meter comprising of consistent 16th note *quintuplets* on the HH, it's safe to assume that one would eventually incorporate accents on downbeats to enhance the feel, sound and presence of the groove. The majority of drummers & instructors utilize and/or teach the usage of the Moeller technique to accurately execute the correct application of the accents. The breakdown of that HH pattern alone would look like this:

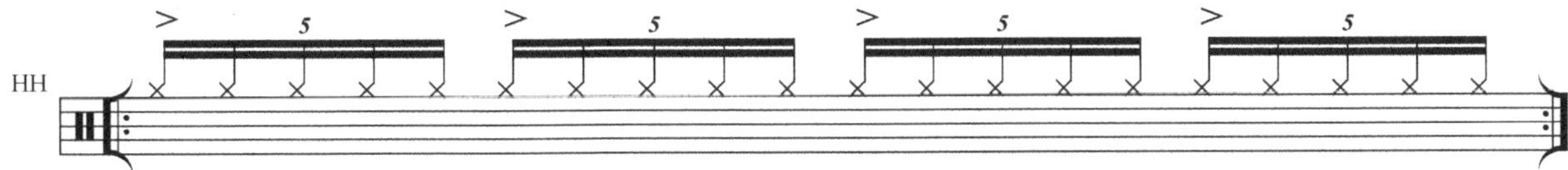

Adding the BD and SD in their proper places to create a "standard groove" with the quintuplet rate, the complete pattern is the one seen here:

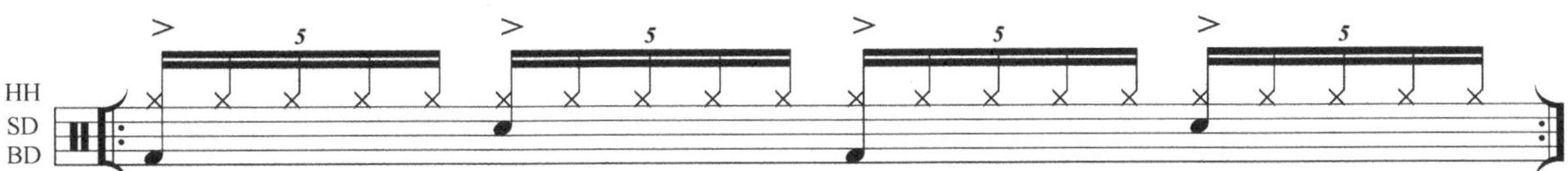

Notice that the above "standard groove" doesn't incorporate any cross rhythmic activity due to the accents laying on downbeats in the beamed groups of "5" and being in sync with the BD & SD pattern. However, in order to start displacing the accents and creating cross rhythmic ideas in a groove setting, a good place to start is to incorporate other numbered groupings in the time hand or limbs. Below is the breakdown of the same HH pattern but now utilizing groupings of "2" to create a cross rhythmic pattern. Take note that the groupings of "2" over a quintuplet rate don't create an "over the bar" rhythm but it does create an "over the beat" rhythm (occurring in the space of every 2 quarter notes).

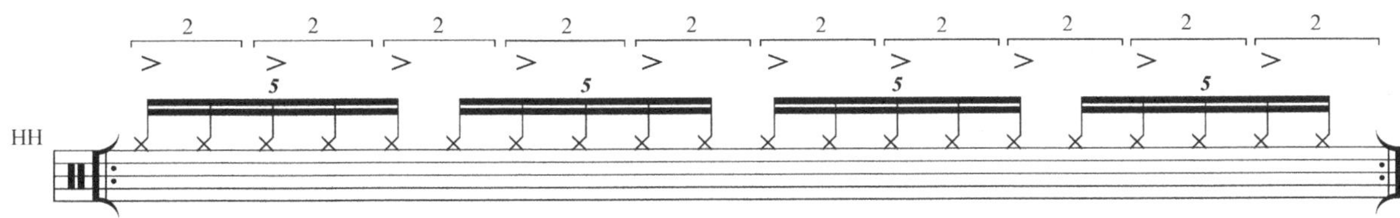

Tip: Counting Exercise

A good suggested exercise for any cross rhythm is to count out loud even before playing as to help build the two existing rhythms internally. Below, you will find a single measure phrase consisting of only 16th note quintuplet note counts, but every 2nd symbol is in **bold** as to represent the placement of an accent. There are several ways of counting quintuplets. A popular method of counting is by using an Indian spoken syllable technique called Konnakol, applying the words "Tha Dhi Gi Na Thom" as each syllabic count. Also, I often find a great method of counting odd-numbered grouping like quintuplets is with a backwards count of "54321." It allows for an evenly-spaced assortment of counts through each quintuplet, though it may take some practice to obtain the flow of the syllables. However to start, let's keep it simple with a standardized method simply using "12345" as your counts. Start by counting out loud, accentuating the bolded symbols while tapping your foot on downbeats in 4/4:

| **1** 2 **3** 4 **5** | 2 **2** 3 **4** 5 | **3** 2 **3** 4 **5** | 4 **2** 3 **4** 5 |

Primary Ostinato

The following pattern you see is the primary hand ostinato which will remain constant through the various grooves & exercises in this section. As your starting point, practice just this hand pattern together to develop independence involved in keeping the accents in groupings of "2" consistent over the top of the snare drum which remains on 2 & 4 throughout.

Practice Note: To obtain the most successful sound & feel of this ostinato, make sure that you are incorporating a repetitive 2-stroke Moeller accent technique in your time hand while you retain a consistent backbeat technique in the snare hand. Make an effort to ensure that the shifting accents do not affect or change the motion in either hand.

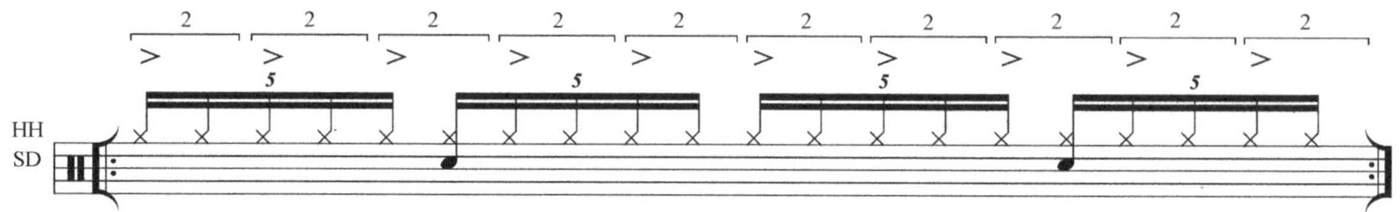

Incorporating the Bass Drum

The final goal is to now complete your phrases & grooves by adding countless bass drum rhythms to the ostinato. A great place to begin is to utilize the "partials," or each individual note of a 16th note quintuplet grouping, one at a time, in your bass drum. Below is the basic quintuplet groove with no accents followed by the same groove with the accents in groupings of "2" over the top in your time hand.

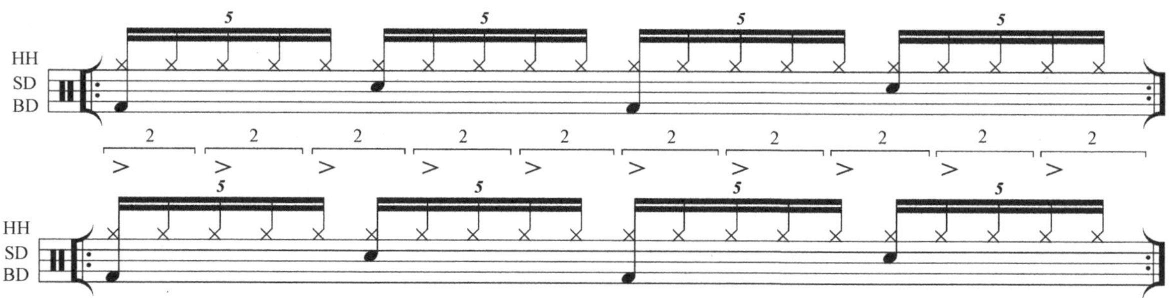

Exercise 33: Quintuplet Partials

Groupings of "2" over a 16th note quintuplet rate with various BD partial combinations

Below, you will find the transcription of the current ostinato once again. The rest of the page contains partials, or "rhythmic portions," of the 16th note quintuplet groupings for you to play in your bass drum. There are 3 ways you can go about working on these exercise pages for independence & variation development:

1) On a separate piece of paper, write out the ostinato 14 times. Extract the 14 rhythms below and insert them one-by-one into the ostinato phrases you've transcribed as bass drum notes.

2) Play & repeat the single-measure ostinato and insert the rhythms below (by ear) into the hand pattern as bass drum notes.

3) If you have a physical copy of the book, simply pencil in a bass drum pattern from a single-measure rhythmic phrase into the ostinato. Once comfortable, erase and then move to transcribing the next rhythms down the page one-by-one.

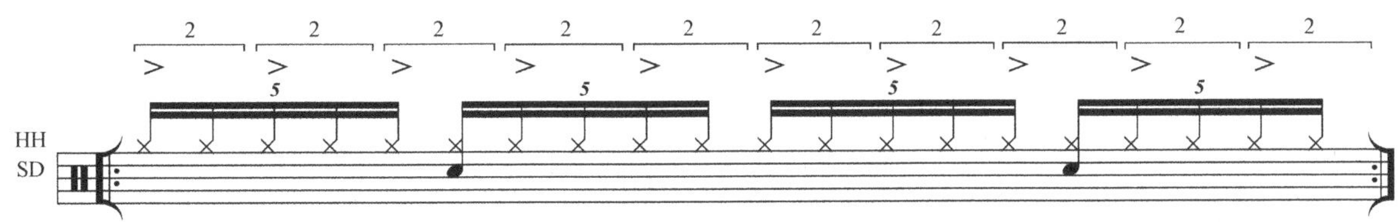

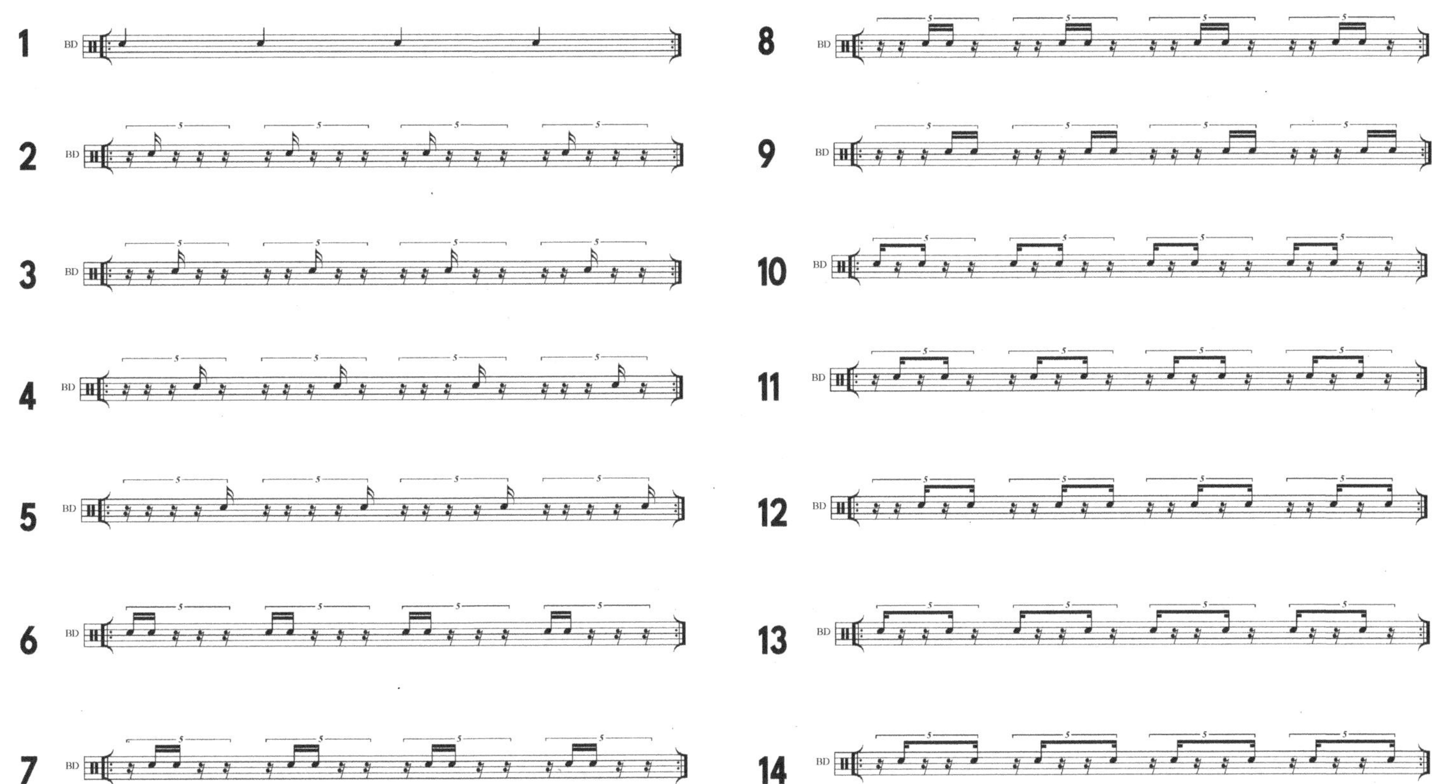

Incorporating a Syncopated Bass Drum Moving Melody

Groupings of "2" over a quintuplet rate

Furthering your independence in varying your bass drum, the next step would be to incorporate variations of 16th note quintuplet partials within an ongoing melody and then combing that with the current ostinato. The melody you will see in the next section is written as if were a snare melody, but you have the option of applying it to any limb that is applied to the kit. As with the previous exercises, we will be applying it to or playing it on the bass drum. An appropriate book to use which displays mixed partials in varied rate groupings is 'Rhythm and Meter Patterns' by Gary Chaffee. The full melody in this section is an example of a page you will find in that book.

Below, find the example of the first measure of the exercise (found on the next page) and how it is then applied to the bass drum under the current ostinato with groupings of "2" in a quintuplet rate. Notice how you're seeing the first measure only of the full melody exercise. Keep in mind that, as in the past few pages, the groupings of "2" over the quintuplet rate only span the length of 2 beats total and reset on the downbeat

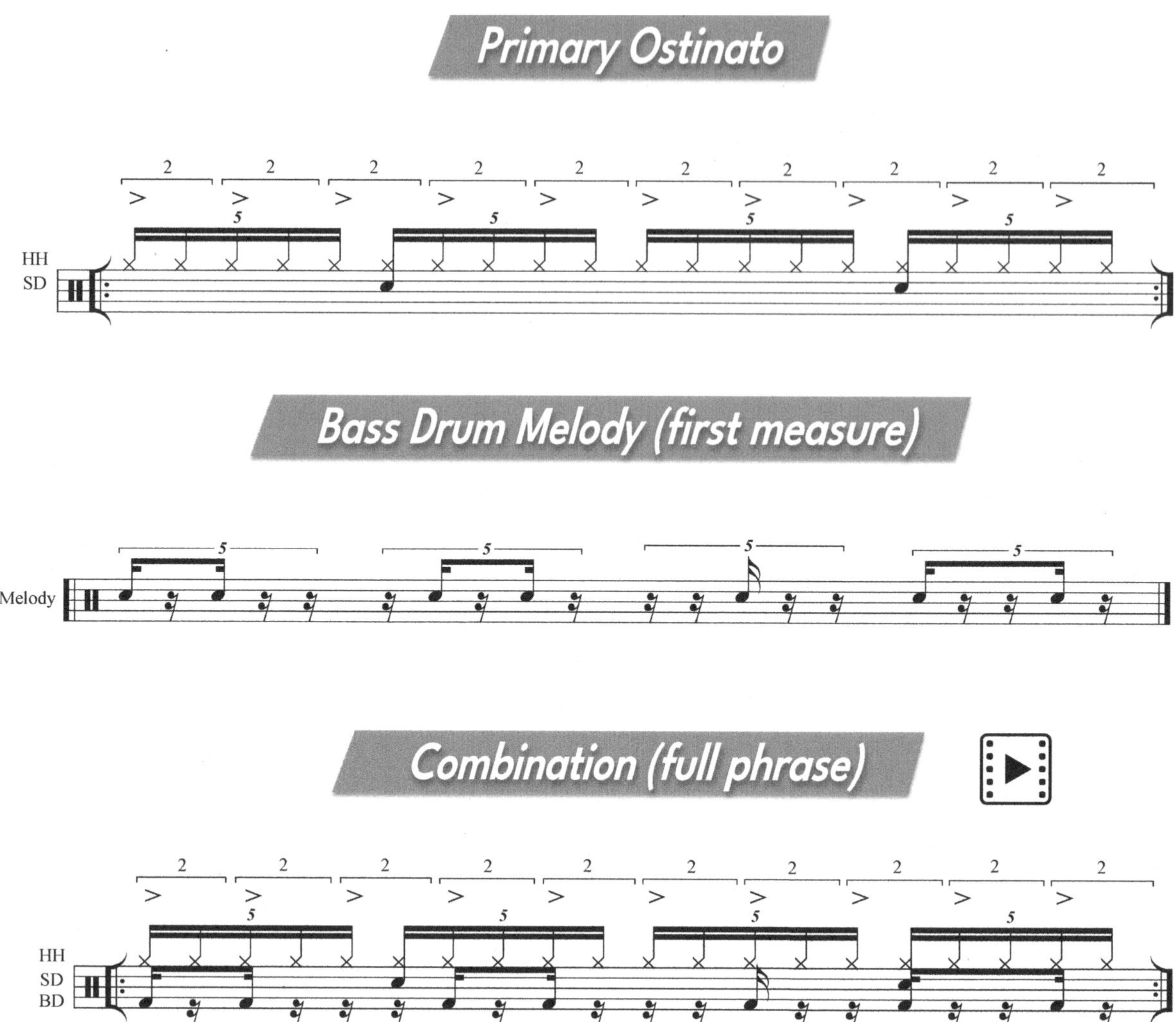

Exercise 34: Syncopated Moving Melody with Quintuplet Partials

16th note quintuplet rate grooves with groupings of "2"

Below, you will find the transcription of the current ostinato once again. The rest of the page contains the entire rhythmic melody that will be applied to the bass drum. There are 3 ways you can go about working on these exercise pages for independence & variation development:

1) On a separate piece of paper, write out the ostinato 12 times. Insert the bass drum notes from the 12 measures of the melody below into the ostinato phrases you've transcribed.

2) Play down the whole exercise/melody and insert the accents (by ear) over the top of the exercise you are playing.

3) If you have a physical copy of the book, simply pencil in 16th note quintuplets over the top of the melody and then write in accents in groupings of "2" over the ongoing quintuplets.

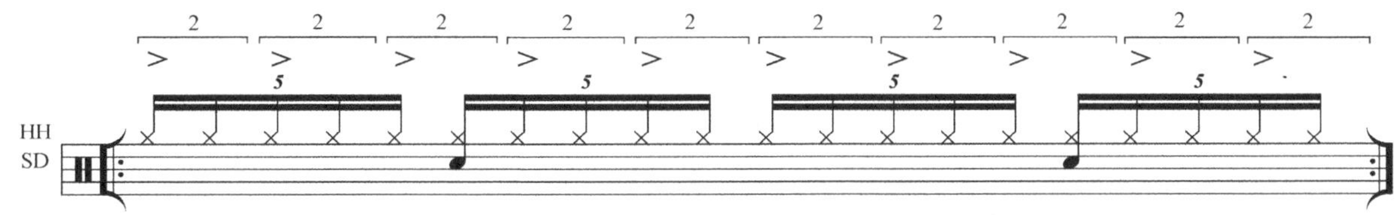

Melody

Section 6 : TUPLETS

Groupings of “3” over a 16th note quintuplet rate in 4/4

In this next portion of the book, the meter will remain in 4/4 and we will still continue the topic of ‘tuplets’ in which the standard rate subdivision of each quarter note (of 2, 4, 8, etc....) expands into alternate choices (3, 5, 7, etc....). This segment of the book introduces the topic of 16th note quintuplets, or groupings beamed in 5 notes, but now with the addition of accents in groupings of “3” over the top.

In a normal 4/4 meter comprising of consistent 16th note *quintuplets* on the HH, it’s safe to assume that one would eventually incorporate accents on downbeats to enhance the feel, sound and presence of the groove. The majority of drummers & instructors utilize and/or teach the usage of the Moeller technique to accurately execute the correct application of the accents. The breakdown of that HH pattern alone would look like this:

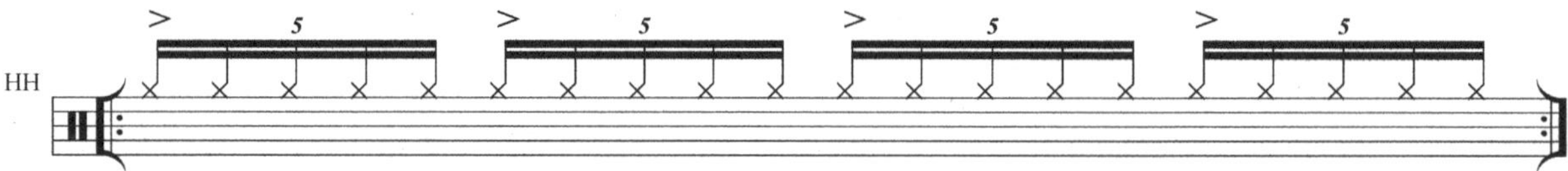

Adding the BD and SD in their proper places to create a “standard groove” with the quintuplet rate, the complete pattern is the one seen here:

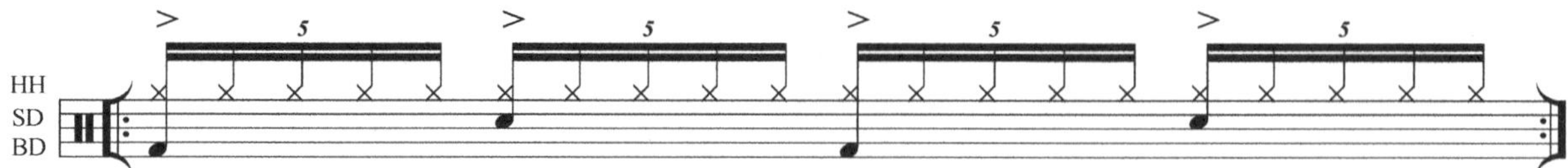

Notice that the above “standard groove” doesn’t incorporate any cross rhythmic activity due to the accents laying on downbeats in the beamed groups of “5” and being in sync with the BD & SD pattern. However, in order to start displacing the accents and creating cross rhythmic ideas in a groove setting, a good place to start is to incorporate other numbered groupings in the time hand or limbs. Below is the breakdown of the same HH pattern but now utilizing groupings of “3” to create a cross rhythmic pattern. Whereas the previous 16th note quintuplet exercises utilizing groupings of “2” did not create an “over the bar” phrase, the usage of accents in groupings of “3” will now create a 3 bar phrase in order to reset again back on beat 1.

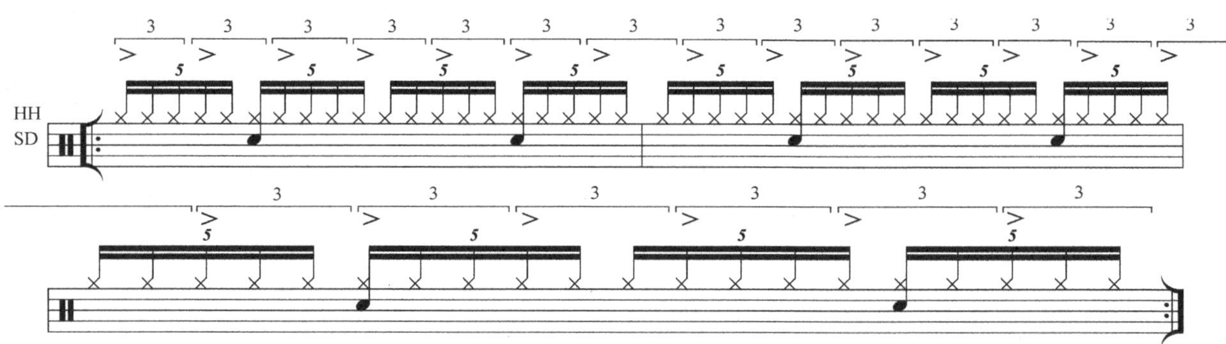

Section 6
Groupings of 3 (Quintuplet rate in 4/4)

Tip: Counting Exercise

A good suggested exercise for any cross rhythm is to count out loud even before playing as to help build the two existing rhythms internally. Below, you will find a 3 measure phrase consisting of only 16th note quintuplet note counts, but every 3rd symbol is in bold as to represent the placement of an accent. There are several ways of counting quintuplets. A popular method of counting is by using an Indian spoken syllable technique called Konnakol, applying the words "Tha Dhi Gi Na Thom" as each syllabic count. Also, I often find a great method of counting odd-numbered grouping like quintuplets is with a backwards count of "54321." It allows for an evenly-spaced assortment of counts through each quintuplet, though it may take some practice to obtain the flow of the syllables. However to start, let's keep it simple with a standardized method simply using "12345" as your counts. Start by counting out loud, accentuating the bolded symbols while tapping your foot on downbeats in 4/4:

| **1** 2 3 **4** 5 | 2 **2** 3 4 **5** | 3 2 **3** 4 5 | **4** 2 3 **4** 5 | 1 **2** 3 4 **5** | 2 2 **3** 4 5 | **3** 2 3 **4** 5 | 4 **2** 3 4 **5** |

| 1 2 **3** 4 5 | **2** 2 3 **4** 5 | 3 **2** 3 4 **5** | 4 2 **3** 4 5 |

Primary Ostinato

The following pattern you see is the primary hand ostinato which will remain constant through the various grooves & exercises in this section. As your starting point, practice just this hand pattern together to develop independence involved in keeping the 16th quintuplet accents in groupings of "3" consistent over the top of the snare drum which remains on 2 & 4 throughout.

Practice Note: To obtain the most successful sound & feel of this ostinato, make sure that you are incorporating a repetitive 3-stroke Moeller accent technique in your time hand while you retain a consistent backbeat technique in the snare hand. Make an effort to ensure that the shifting accents do not affect or change the motion in either hand.

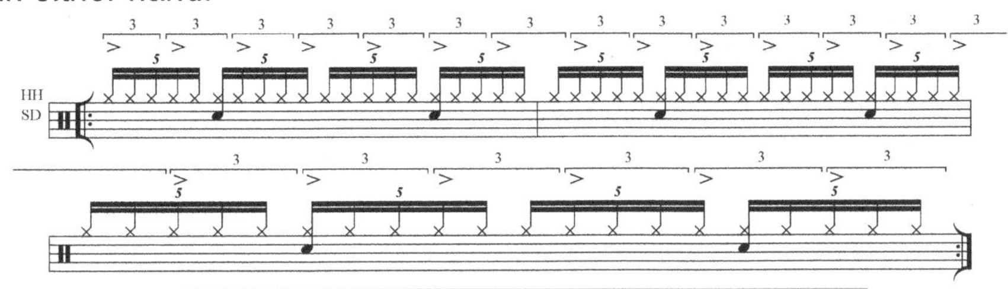

Incorporating the Bass Drum

The final goal is to now complete your phrases & grooves by adding countless bass drum rhythms to the ostinato. A great place to begin is to utilize the "partials," or each individual note of a 16th note quintuplet grouping, one at a time, in your bass drum. Below is the basic quintuplet groove with no accents followed by the same groove with the accents in groupings of "3" over the top in your time hand.

Exercise 35: Quintuplet Partials

Groupings of "3" over a 16th note quintuplet rate with various BD partial combinations

Below, you will find the transcription of the current ostinato once again. The rest of the page contains partials, or "rhythmic portions," of the 16th note quintuplet groupings for you to play in your bass drum. There are 3 ways you can go about working on these exercise pages for independence & variation development:

1) On a separate piece of paper, write out the ostinato 14 times. Extract the 14 rhythms below and insert them one-by-one into the ostinato phrases you've transcribed as bass drum notes.

2) Play & repeat the single-measure ostinato and insert the rhythms below (by ear) into the hand pattern as bass drum notes.

3) If you have a physical copy of the book, simply pencil in a bass drum pattern from a single-measure rhythmic phrase 3 times into the ostinato. Once comfortable, erase and then move to transcribing the next rhythms down the page one-by-one.

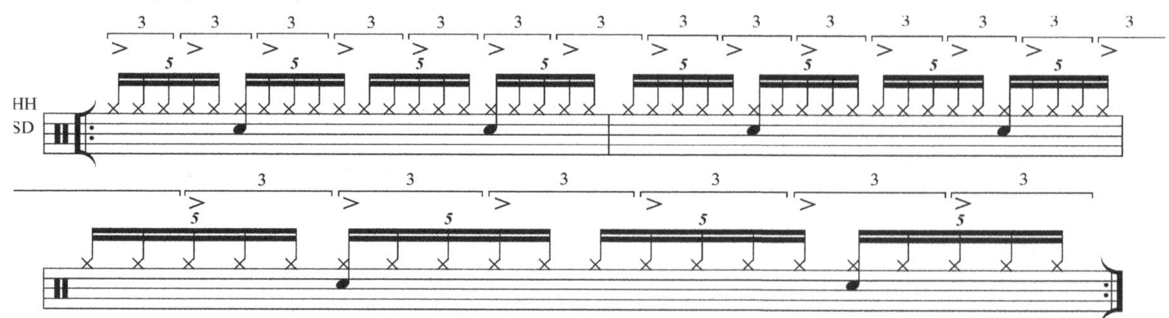

1 BD

2 BD

3 BD

4 BD

5 BD

6 BD

7 BD

8 BD

9 BD

10 BD

11 BD

12 BD

13 BD

14 BD

Incorporating a Syncopated Bass Drum Moving Melody

Groupings of "3" over a quintuplet rate

Furthering your independence in varying your bass drum, the next step would be to incorporate variations of 16th note quintuplet partials within an ongoing melody and then combing that with the current ostinato. The melody you will see in the next section is written as if were a snare melody, but you have the option of applying it to any limb that is applied to the kit. As with the previous exercises, we will be applying it to or playing it on the bass drum. An appropriate book to use which displays mixed partials in varied rate groupings is *Rhythm and Meter Patterns* by Gary Chaffee. The full melody in this section is an example of a page you will find in that book.

Below, find the example of the first 3 measures of the exercise (found on the next page) and how it is then applied to the bass drum under the current ostinato with groupings of "3" in a quintuplet rate. Notice how you're seeing the first three measures only of the full melody exercise. Keep in mind that the groupings of "3" over the 16th note quintuplet rate will create 3 bar phrases total in order to come back to your starting point of beat 1. Below, find the process of assembling the bass drum melody with the ostinato.

Primary Ostinato

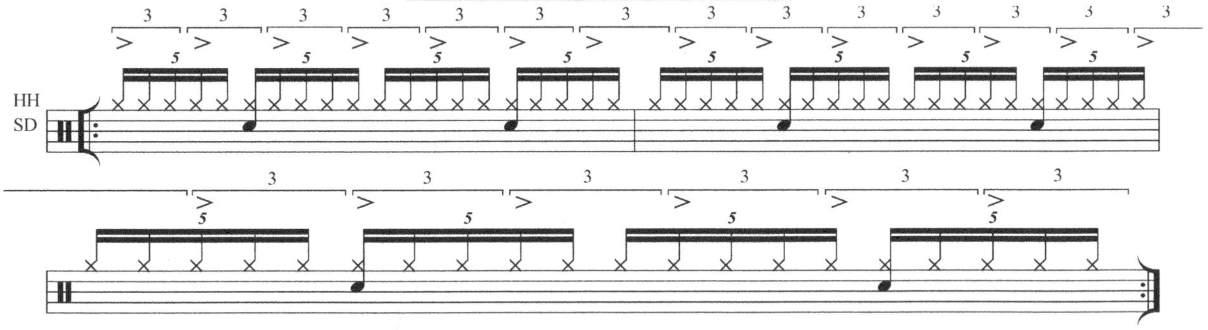

HH
SD

Bass Drum Melody (first 3 measures)

Melody

Combination (full phrase)

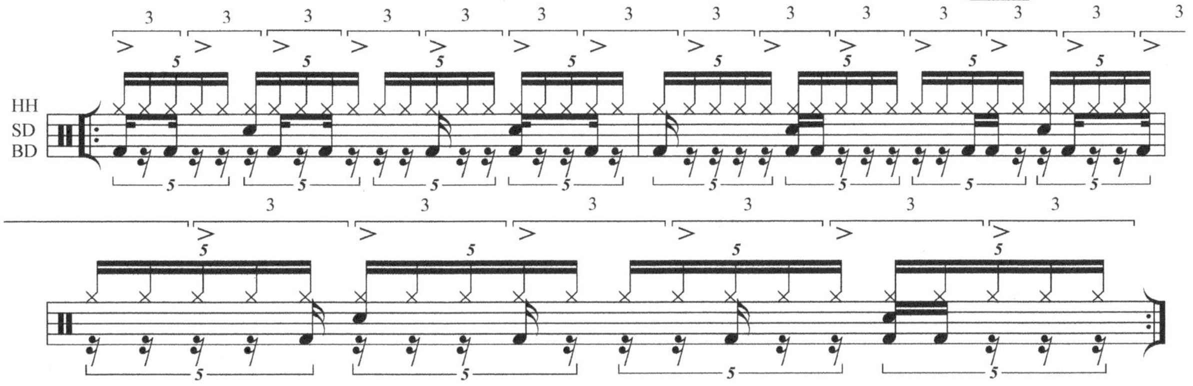

HH
SD
BD

Exercise 36: Syncopated Moving Melody with Quintuplet Partials

16th note quintuplet rate grooves with groupings of "3"

Below, you will find the transcription of the current ostinato once again. The rest of the page contains the entire rhythmic melody that will be applied to the bass drum. There are 3 ways you can go about working on these exercise pages for independence & variation development:

1) On a separate piece of paper, write out the ostinato 4 times. Insert the bass drum notes from the 12 measures of the melody below into the ostinato phrases you've transcribed.

2) Play down the whole exercise/melody and insert the accents (by ear) over the top of the exercise you are playing.

3) If you have a physical copy of the book, simply pencil in 16th note quintuplets over the top of the melody and then write in accents in groupings of "3" over the ongoing quintuplets.

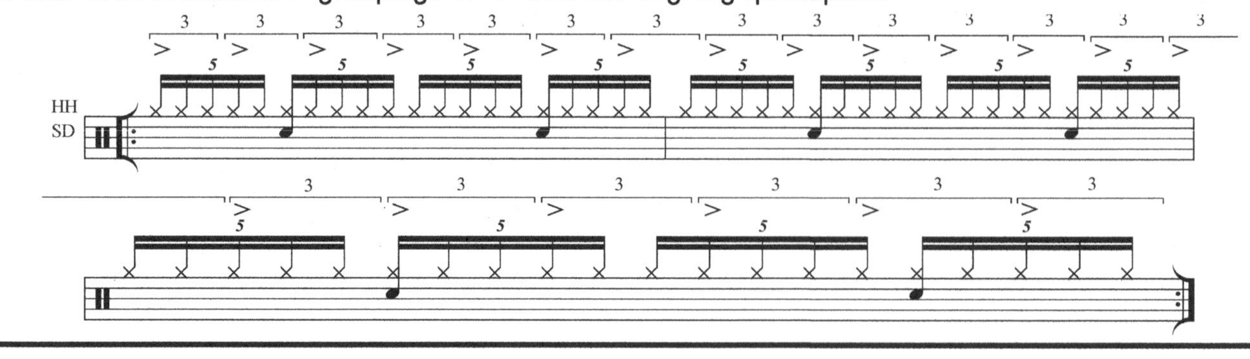

*Asterisks designate the measures where the accented groupings & phrases of "3" will reset on beat 1 again

Section 7: TUPLETS

Groupings of "4" over a 16th note quintuplet rate in 4/4

In this next portion of the book, the meter will remain in 4/4 and we will still continue the topic of 'tuplets' in which the standard rate subdivision of each quarter note (of 2, 4, 8, etc....) expands into alternate choices (3, 5, 7, etc....). This segment of the book introduces the topic of 16th note quintuplets, or groupings beamed in 5 notes, but now with the addition of accents in groupings of "4" over the top.

In a normal 4/4 meter comprising of consistent 16th note *quintuplets* on the HH, it's safe to assume that one would eventually incorporate accents on downbeats to enhance the feel, sound and presence of the groove. The majority of drummers & instructors utilize and/or teach the usage of the Moeller technique to accurately execute the correct application of the accents. The breakdown of that HH pattern alone would look like this:

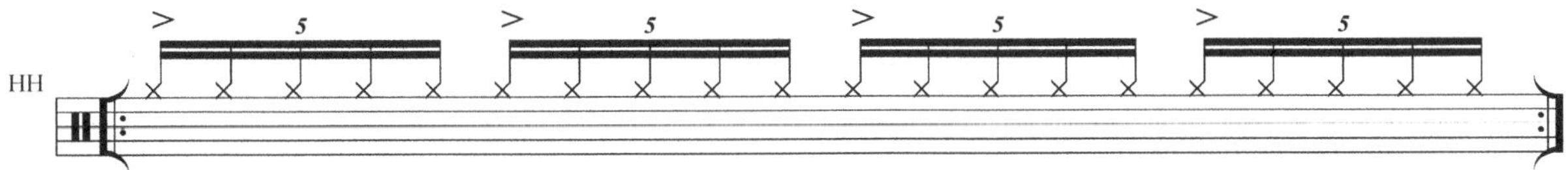

Adding the BD and SD in their proper places to create a "standard groove" with the quintuplet rate, the complete pattern is the one seen here:

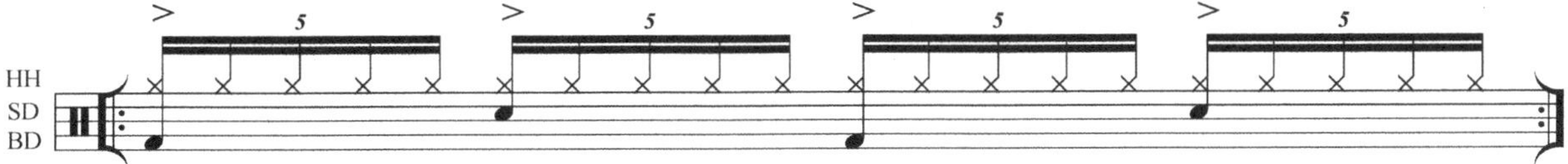

Notice that the above "standard groove" doesn't incorporate any cross rhythmic activity due to the accents laying on downbeats in the beamed groups of "5" and being in sync with the BD & SD pattern. However, in order to start displacing the accents and creating cross rhythmic ideas in a groove setting, a good place to start is to incorporate other numbered groupings in the time hand or limbs. Below is the breakdown of the same HH pattern but now utilizing groupings of "4" to create a cross rhythmic pattern. Take note that, similar to the groupings of "2," the groupings of "4" over a quintuplet rate don't create an "over the bar" rhythm but it does create an "over the beat" rhythm.

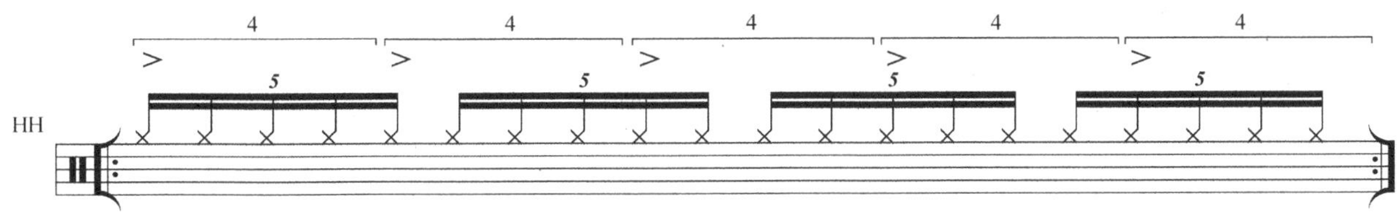

***Tip*: Counting Exercise**

A good suggested exercise for any cross rhythm is to count out loud even before playing as to help build the two existing rhythms internally. Below, you will find a single measure phrase consisting of only 16th note quintuplet note counts, but every 4th symbol is in **bold** as to represent the placement of an accent. There are several ways of counting quintuplets. A popular method of counting is by using an Indian spoken syllable technique called Konnakol, applying the words "Tha Dhi Gi Na Thom" as each syllabic count. Also, I often find a great method of counting odd-numbered grouping like quintuplets is with a backwards count of "54321." It allows for an evenly-spaced assortment of counts through each quintuplet, though it may take some practice to obtain the flow of the syllables. However to start, let's keep it simple with a standardized method simply using "12345" as your counts. Start by counting out loud, accentuating the bolded symbols while tapping your foot on downbeats in 4/4:

| **1** 2 3 4 **5** | 2 2 3 **4** 5 | 3 2 **3** 4 5 | 4 **2** 3 4 5 |

Primary Ostinato

The following pattern you see is the primary hand ostinato which will remain constant through the various grooves & exercises in this section. As your starting point, practice just this hand pattern together to develop independence involved in keeping the accents in groupings of "4" consistent over the top of the snare drum which remains on 2 & 4 throughout.

***Practice Note*:** To obtain the most successful sound & feel of this ostinato, make sure that you are incorporating a repetitive 4-stroke Moeller accent technique in your time hand while you retain a consistent backbeat technique in the snare hand. Make an effort to ensure that the shifting accents do not affect or change the motion in either hand.

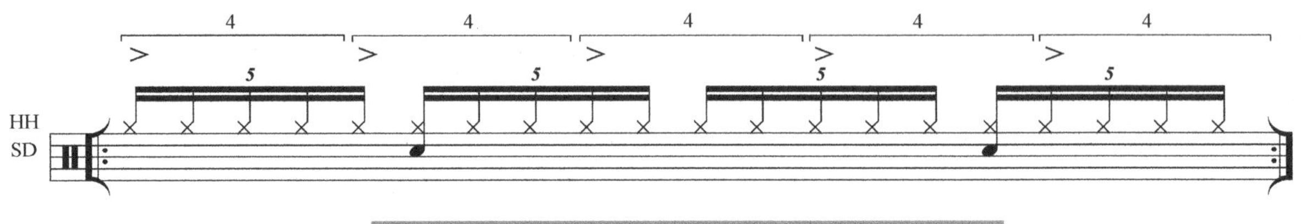

Incorporating the Bass Drum

The final goal is to now complete your phrases & grooves by adding countless bass drum rhythms to the ostinato. A great place to begin is to utilize the "partials," or each individual note of a 16th note quintuplet grouping, one at a time, in your bass drum. Below is the basic quintuplet groove with no accents followed by the same groove with the accents in groupings of "4" over the top in your time hand.

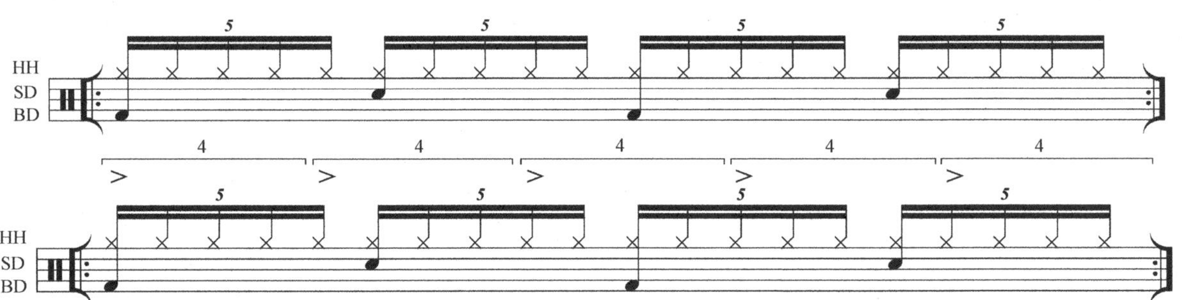

Exercise 37: Quintuplet Partials

Groupings of "4" over a 16th note quintuplet rate with various BD partial combinations

Below, you will find the transcription of the current ostinato once again. The rest of the page contains partials, or "rhythmic portions," of the 16th note quintuplet groupings for you to play in your bass drum. There are 3 ways you can go about working on these exercise pages for independence & variation development:

1) On a separate piece of paper, write out the ostinato 14 times. Extract the 14 rhythms below and insert them one-by-one into the ostinato phrases you've transcribed as bass drum notes.

2) Play & repeat the single-measure ostinato and insert the rhythms below (by ear) into the hand pattern as bass drum notes.

3) If you have a physical copy of the book, simply pencil in a bass drum pattern from a single-measure rhythmic phrase into the ostinato. Once comfortable, erase and then move to transcribing the next rhythms down the page one-by-one.

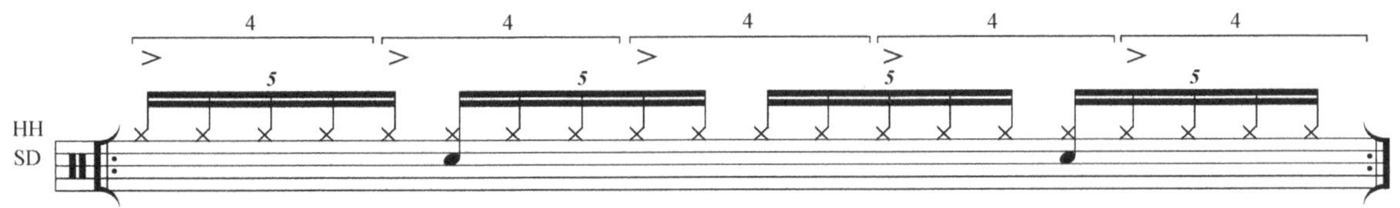

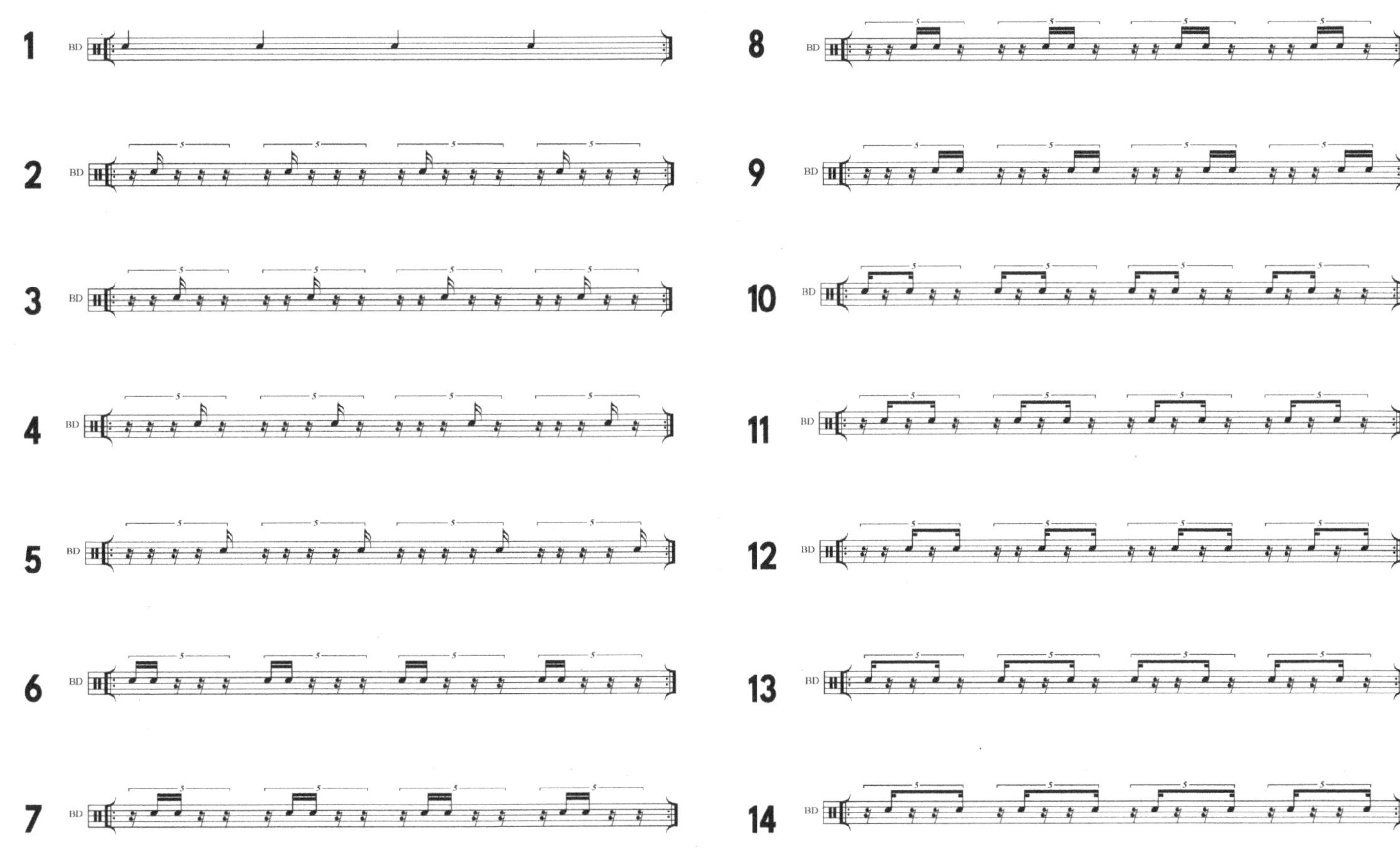

Incorporating a Syncopated Bass Drum Moving Melody

Groupings of "4" over a quintuplet rate

Furthering your independence in varying your bass drum, the next step would be to incorporate variations of 16th note quintuplet partials within an ongoing melody and then combing that with the current ostinato. The melody you will see in the next section is written as if were a snare melody, but you have the option of applying it to any limb that is applied to the kit. As with the previous exercises, we will be applying it to or playing it on the bass drum. An appropriate book to use which displays mixed partials in varied rate groupings is *Rhythm and Meter Patterns* by Gary Chaffee. The full melody in this section is an example of a page you will find in that book.

Below, find the example of the first measure of the exercise (found on the next page) and how it is then applied to the bass drum under the current ostinato with groupings of "4" in a quintuplet rate. Notice how you're seeing the first measure only of the full melody exercise. Keep in mind that, as with the groupings of "2" over the quintuplet rate, the groupings of "4" only span the length of 1 measure total and reset on the downbeat of each measure. Below, find the process of assembling the bass drum melody with the ostinato.

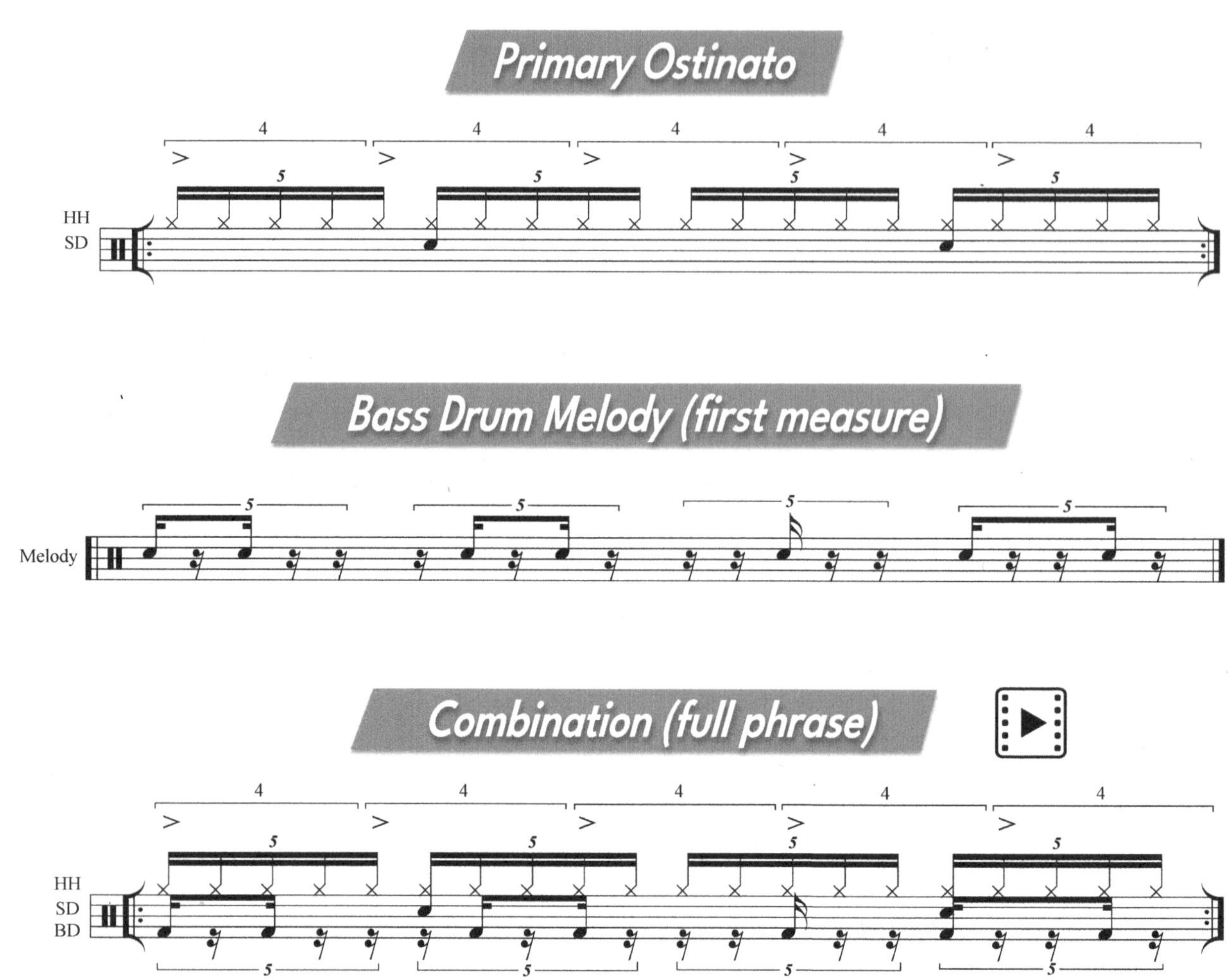

Exercise 38: Syncopated Moving Melody with Quintuplet Partials

16th note quintuplet rate grooves with groupings of "4"

Below, you will find the transcription of the current ostinato once again. The rest of the page contains the entire rhythmic melody that will be applied to the bass drum. There are 3 ways you can go about working on these exercise pages for independence & variation development:

1) On a separate piece of paper, write out the ostinato 12 times. Insert the bass drum notes from the 12 measures of the melody below into the ostinato phrases you've transcribed.

2) Play down the whole exercise/melody and insert the accents (by ear) over the top of the exercise you are playing.

3) If you have a physical copy of the book, simply pencil in 16th note quintuplets over the top of the melody and then write in accents in groupings of "4" over the ongoing quintuplets.

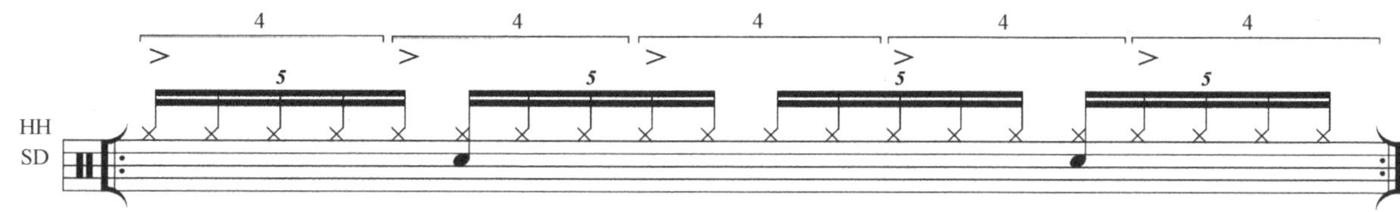

Melody

Section 8: TUPLETS

Groupings of "2" over a 16th note septuplet rate in 4/4

In this portion of the book, the meter will still remain in 4/4. However, this next section builds upon the current topics that have recently been explored. Continuing the topic of 'tuplets' in which the standard rate subdivision of each quarter note (of 2, 4, 8, etc....) expand into alternate choices (3, 5, 7, etc....), this segment of the book introduces the topic of 16th note septuplets, or groupings beamed in 7 notes.

In a normal 4/4 meter comprising of consistent 16th note *septuplets* on the HH, it's safe to assume that one would eventually incorporate accents on downbeats to enhance the feel, sound and presence of the groove. The majority of drummers & instructors utilize and/or teach the usage of the Moeller technique to accurately execute the correct application of the accents. The breakdown of that HH pattern alone would look like this:

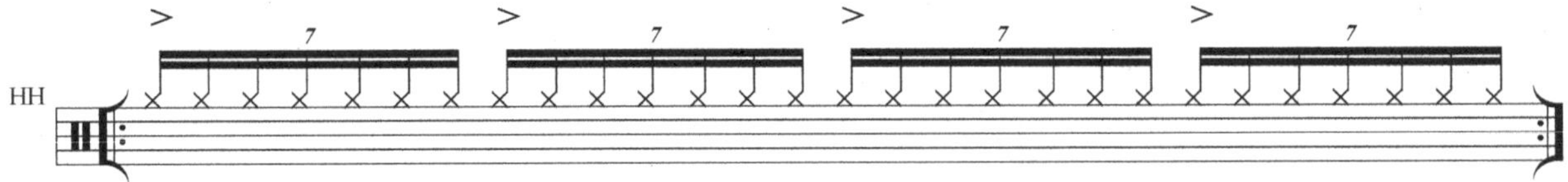

Adding the BD and SD in their proper places to create a "standard groove" with the septuplet rate, the complete pattern is the one seen here:

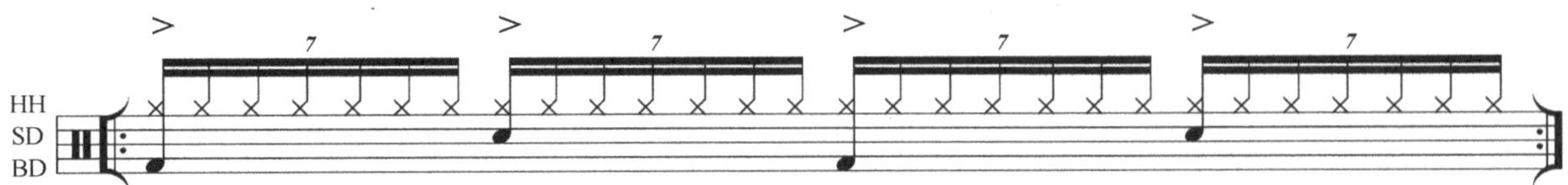

Notice that the above "standard groove" doesn't incorporate any cross rhythmic activity due to the accents laying on downbeats in the beamed groups of "7" and being in sync with the BD & SD pattern. However, in order to start displacing the accents and creating cross rhythmic ideas in a groove setting, a good place to start is to incorporate other numbered groupings in the time hand or limbs. Below is the breakdown of the same HH pattern but now utilizing groupings of "2" to create a cross rhythmic pattern. Take note that the groupings of "2" over a septuplet rate don't create an "over the bar" rhythm but it does create an "over the beat" rhythm (occurring in the space of every 2 quarter notes).

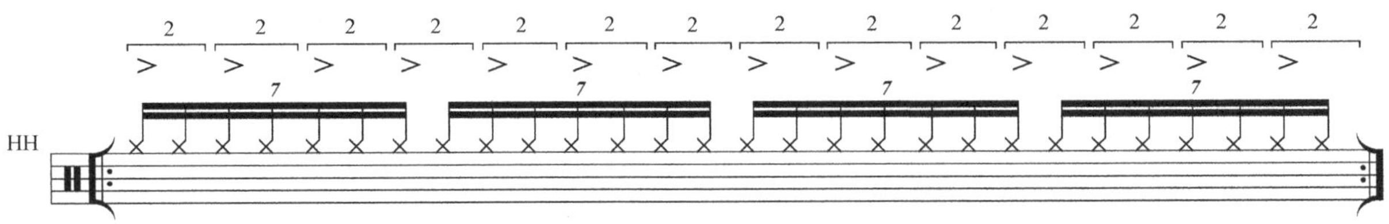

Tip: Counting Exercise

A good suggested exercise for any cross rhythm is to count out loud even before playing as to help build the two existing rhythms internally. Below, you will find a single measure phrase consisting of only 16th note septuplet note counts, but every 2nd symbol is in **bold** as to represent the placement of an accent. There are several ways of counting septuplets. A popular method of counting is by using an Indian spoken syllable technique called Konnakol, applying the words "Ta Ka Di Mi Ta Ki Ta" as each syllabic count. Also, I often find a great method of counting odd-numbered grouping like septuplets is with a backwards count of "7654321." It allows for an evenly-spaced assortment of counts through each septuplet, though it may take some practice to obtain the flow of the syllables. However to start, let's keep it simple with a standardized method simply using "1234567" as your counts. Start by counting out loud, accentuating the bolded symbols while tapping your foot on downbeats in 4/4:

| **1** 2 **3** 4 **5** 6 **7** | 2 **2** 3 **4** 5 **6** 7 | **3** 2 **3** 4 **5** 6 **7** | 4 **2** 3 **4** 5 **6** 7 |

Primary Ostinato

The following pattern you see is the primary hand ostinato which will remain constant through the various grooves & exercises in this section. As your starting point, practice just this hand pattern together to develop independence involved in keeping the accents in groupings of "2" consistent over the top of the snare drum which remains on 2 & 4 throughout.

Practice Note: To obtain the most successful sound & feel of this ostinato, make sure that you are incorporating a repetitive 2-stroke Moeller accent technique in your time hand while you retain a consistent backbeat technique in the snare hand. Make an effort to ensure that the shifting accents do not affect or change the motion in either hand.

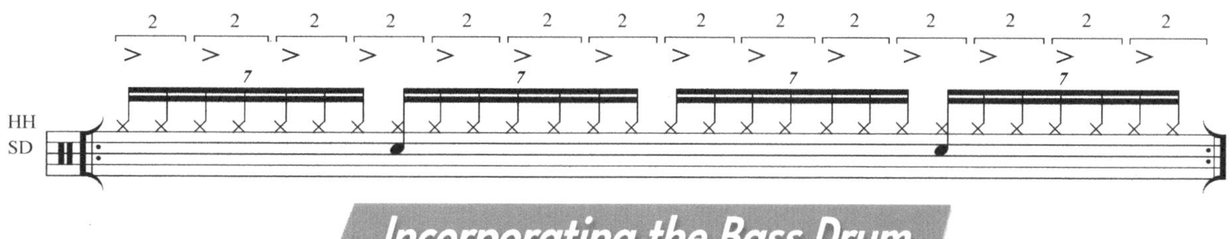

Incorporating the Bass Drum

The final goal is to now complete your phrases & grooves by adding countless bass drum rhythms to the ostinato. A great place to begin is to utilize the "partials," or each individual note of a 16th note septuplet grouping, one at a time, in your bass drum. Below is the basic septuplet groove with no accents followed by the same groove with the accents in groupings of "2" over the top in your time hand.

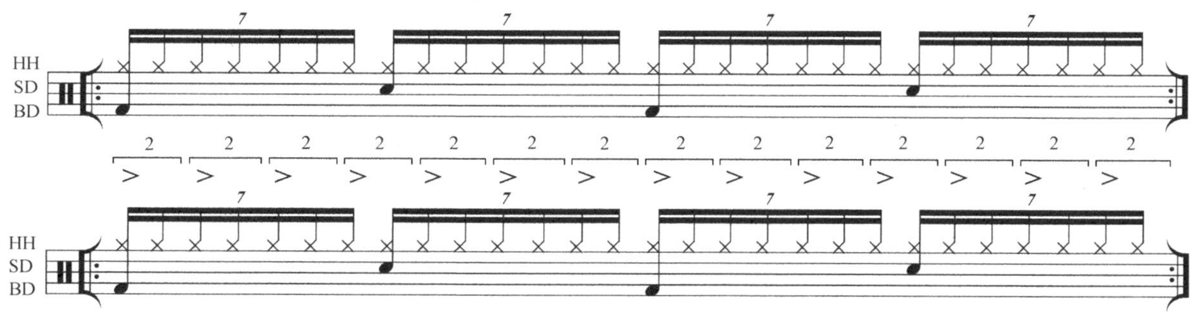

Exercise 39: Septuplet Partials

Groupings of "2" over a 16th note septuplet rate with various BD partial combinations

Below, you will find the transcription of the current ostinato once again. The rest of the page contains partials, or "rhythmic portions," of the 16th note septuplet groupings for you to play in your bass drum. There are 3 ways you can go about working on these exercise pages for independence & variation development:

1) On a separate piece of paper, write out the ostinato 14 times. Extract 14 rhythms below and insert them one-by-one into the ostinato phrases you've transcribed as bass drum notes.

2) Play & repeat the single-measure ostinato and insert the rhythms below (by ear) into the hand pattern as bass drum notes.

3) If you have a physical copy of the book, simply pencil in a bass drum pattern from a single-measure rhythmic phrase into the ostinato. Once comfortable, erase and then move to transcribing the next rhythms down the page one-by-one.

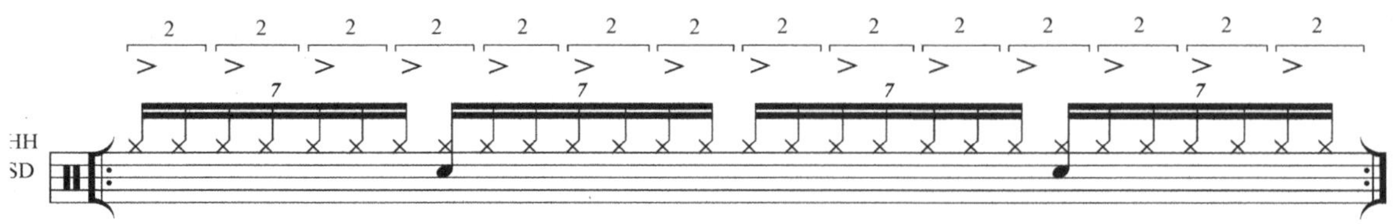

1 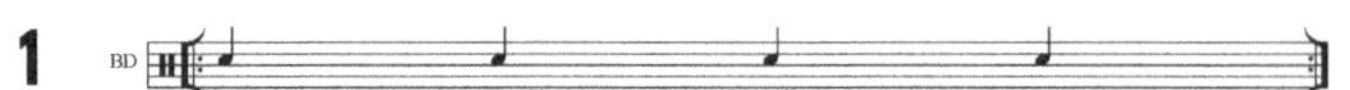

2

3

4

5

6

7

8

9 

10

11

12

13

14

Incorporating a Syncopated Bass Drum Moving Melody

Groupings of “2” over a septuplet rate

Furthering your independence in varying your bass drum, the next step would be to incorporate variations of 16th note septuplet partials within an ongoing melody and then combing that with the current ostinato. The melody you will see in the next section is written as if were a snare melody, but you have the option of applying it to any limb that is applied to the kit. As with the previous exercises, we will be applying it to or playing it on the bass drum. An appropriate book to use which displays mixed partials in varied rate groupings is ‘Rhythm and Meter Patterns’ by Gary Chaffee. The full melody in this section is an example of a page you may find in that book.

Below, find the example of the first measure of the exercise (found on the next page) and how it is then applied to the bass drum under the current ostinato with groupings of “2” in a septuplet rate. Notice how you’re seeing the first measure only of the full melody exercise. Keep in mind that, as in the past few pages, the groupings of “2” over the septuplet rate only span the length of 2 beats total and reset on the downbeat of each measure. Below, find the process of assembling the bass drum melody with the ostinato.

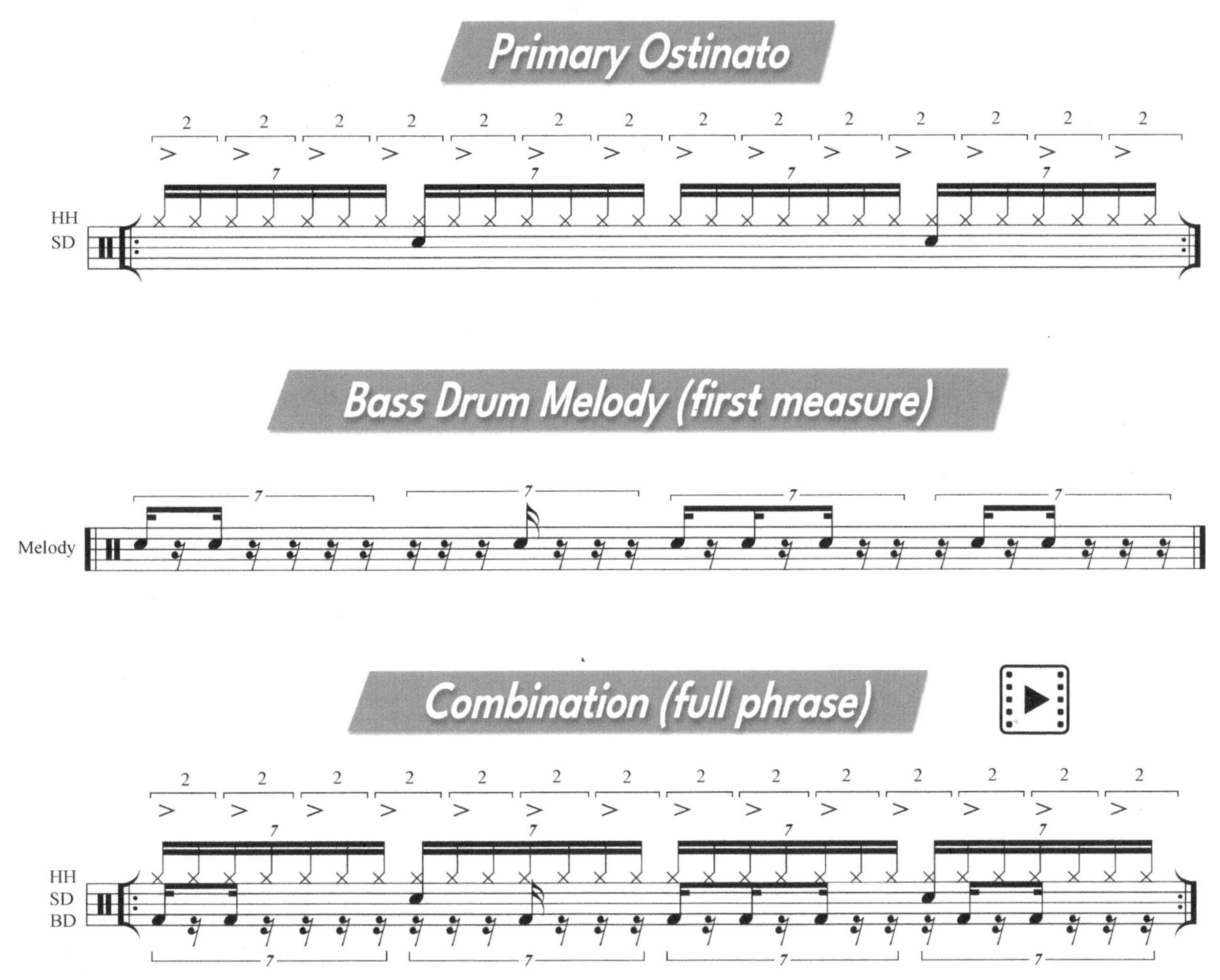

Exercise 40 : Syncopated Moving Melody with Septuplet Partials

16th note septuplet rate grooves with groupings of "2"

Below, you will find the transcription of the current ostinato once again. The rest of the page contains the entire rhythmic melody that will be applied to the bass drum. There are 3 ways you can go about working on these exercise pages for independence & variation development:

1) On a separate piece of paper, write out the ostinato 12 times. Insert the bass drum notes from the 12 measures of the melody below into the ostinato phrases you've transcribed.

2) Play down the whole exercise/melody and insert the accents (by ear) over the top of the exercise you are playing.

3) If you have a physical copy of the book, simply pencil in 16th note septuplets over the top of the melody and then write in accents in groupings of "2" over the ongoing septuplets.

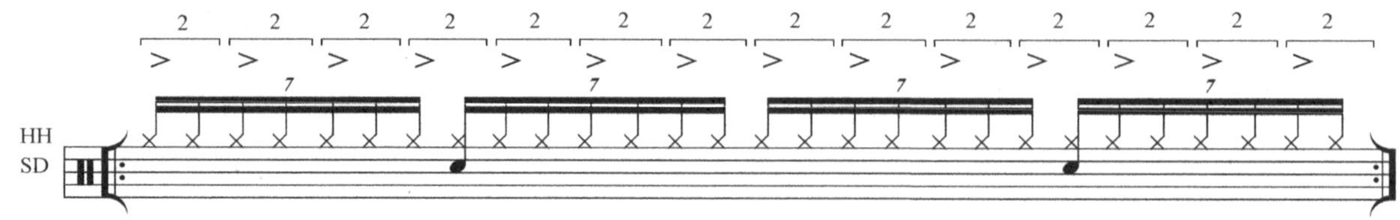

Melody

Section 9 : TUPLETS

Groupings of "3" over a 16th note septuplet rate in 4/4

In this portion of the book, the meter will still remain in 4/4. As in previous pages, this next section builds upon the current topics that have recently been explored. Continuing the topic of 'tuplets' in which the standard rate subdivision of each quarter note (of 2, 4, 8, etc....) expand into alternate choices (3, 5, 7, etc....), this segment of the book continues the topic of 16th note septuplets, or groupings beamed in 7 notes.

In a normal 4/4 meter comprising of consistent 16th note septuplets on the HH, it's safe to assume that one would eventually incorporate accents on downbeats to enhance the feel, sound and presence of the groove. The majority of drummers & instructors utilize and/or teach the usage of the Moeller technique to accurately execute the correct application of the accents. The breakdown of that HH pattern alone would look like this:

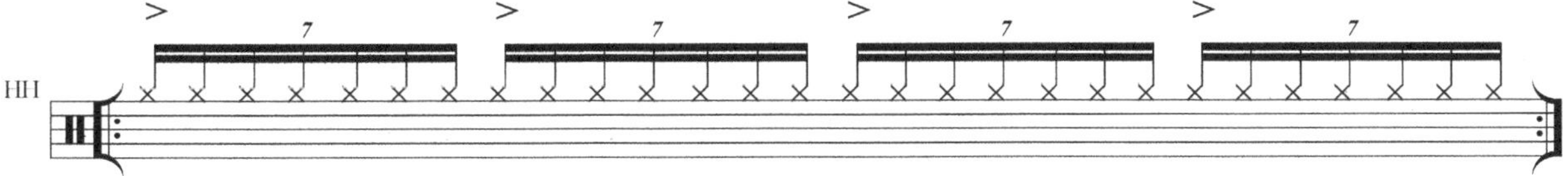

Adding the BD and SD in their proper places to create a "standard groove" with the septuplet rate, the complete pattern is the one seen here:

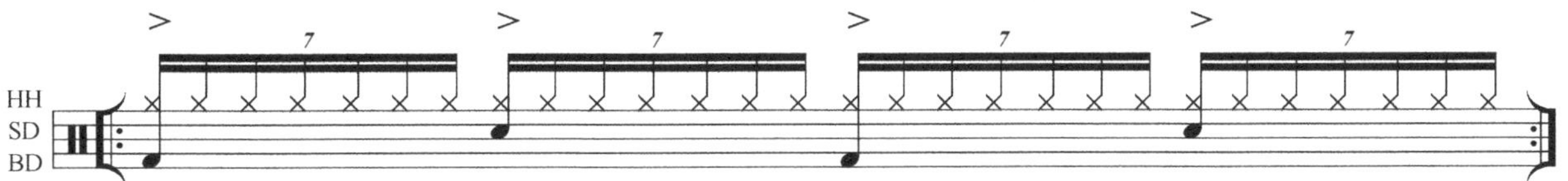

Notice that the above "standard groove" doesn't incorporate any cross rhythmic activity due to the accents laying on downbeats in the beamed groups of "7" and being in sync with the BD & SD pattern. However, in order to start displacing the accents and creating cross rhythmic ideas in a groove setting, the next place to start is to incorporate other numbered groupings in the time hand or limbs. Below is the breakdown of the same HH pattern but now utilizing groupings of "3" to create a cross rhythmic pattern. Whereas the previous 16th note septuplet exercises utilizing groupings of "2" did not create an "over the bar" phrase, the usage of accents in groupings of "3" will now create a 3 bar phrase in order to reset again back on beat 1.

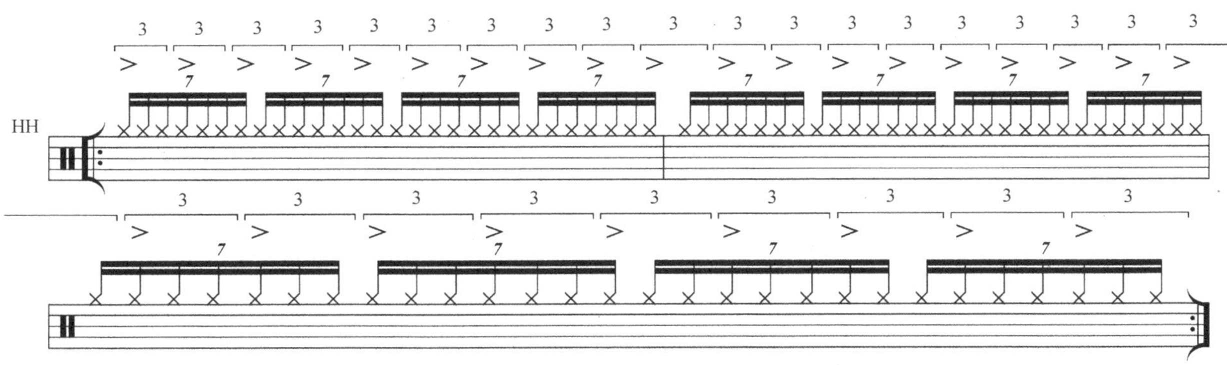

Tip: Counting Exercise

A good suggested exercise for any cross rhythm is to count out loud even before playing as to help build the two existing rhythms internally. Below, you will find a 3 measure phrase consisting of only 16th note septuplet note counts, but every 3rd symbol is in **bold** as to represent the placement of an accent. There are several ways of counting septuplets. A popular method of counting is by using an Indian spoken syllable technique called Konnakol, applying the words "Ta Ka Di Mi Ta Ki Ta" as each syllabic count. Also, I often find a great method of counting odd-numbered grouping like septuplets is with a backwards count of "7654321." It allows for an evenly-spaced assortment of counts through each septuplet, though it may take some practice to obtain the flow of the syllables. However to start, let's keep it simple with a standardized method simply using "1234567" as your counts. Start by counting out loud, accentuating the bolded symbols while tapping your foot on downbeats in 4/4:

| **1** 2 3 **4** 5 6 **7** | 2 2 **3** 4 5 **6** 7 | 3 **2** 3 4 **5** 6 7 | **4** 2 3 **4** 5 6 **7** | 1 2 **3** 4 5 **6** 7 | 2 **2** 3 4 **5** 6 7 | **3** 2 3 **4** 5 6 **7** | 4 2 **3** 4 5 **6** 7 |

| 1 **2** 3 4 **5** 6 7 | **2** 2 3 **4** 5 6 **7** | 3 2 **3** 4 5 **6** 7 | 4 **2** 3 4 **5** 6 7 |

Primary Ostinato

The following pattern you see is the primary hand ostinato which will remain constant through the various grooves & exercises in this section. As your starting point, practice just this hand pattern together to develop independence involved in keeping the accents in groupings of "3" consistent over the top of the snare drum which remains on 2 & 4 throughout.

Practice Note: To obtain the most successful sound & feel of this ostinato, make sure that you are incorporating a repetitive 3-stroke Moeller accent technique in your time hand while you retain a consistent backbeat technique in the snare hand. Make an effort to ensure that the shifting accents do not affect or change the motion in either hand.

Incorporating the Bass Drum

The final goal is to now complete your phrases & grooves by adding countless bass drum rhythms to the ostinato. A great place to begin is to utilize the "partials," or each individual note of a 16th note septuplet grouping, one at a time, in your bass drum. Below is the basic septuplet groove with no accents followed by the same groove with the accents in groupings of "3" over the top in your time hand.

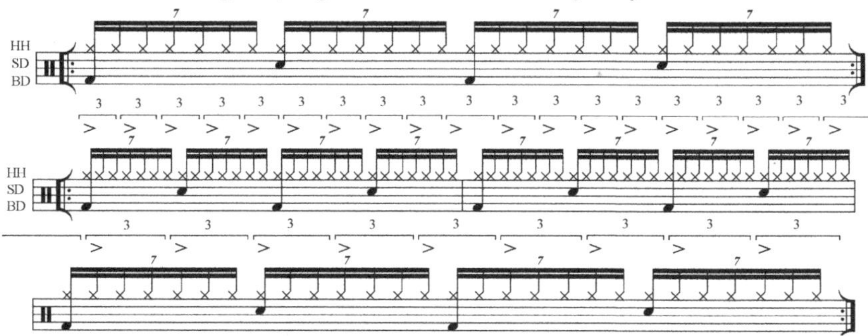

Exercise 41: Septuplet Partials

Groupings of "3" over a 16th note septuplet rate with various BD partial combinations

Below, you will find the transcription of the current ostinato once again. The rest of the page contains partials, or "rhythmic portions," of the 16th note septuplet groupings for you to play in your bass drum. There are 3 ways you can go about working on these exercise pages for independence & variation development:

1) On a separate piece of paper, write out the ostinato 14 times. Extract 14 rhythms below and insert them one-by-one into the ostinato phrases you've transcribed as bass drum notes.

2) Play & repeat the three-measure ostinato and insert the rhythms below (by ear) into the hand pattern as bass drum notes.

3) If you have a physical copy of the book, simply pencil in a bass drum pattern from a single-measure rhythmic phrase 3 times into the ostinato. Once comfortable, erase and then move to transcribing the next rhythms down the page one-by-one.

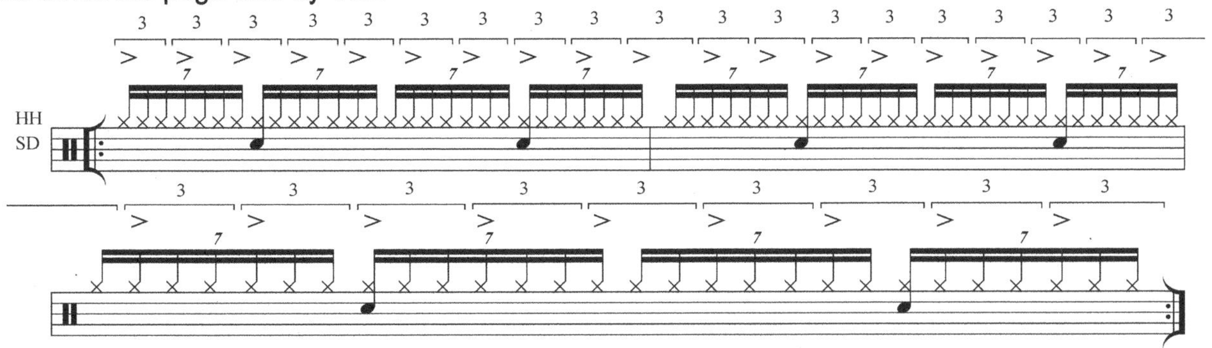

1 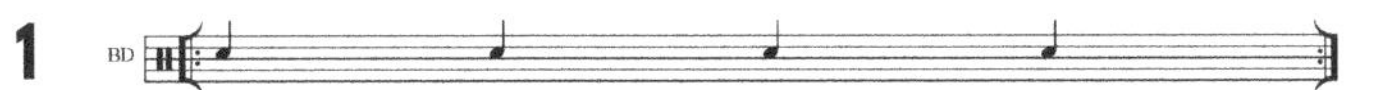

2

3

4

5

6

7

8 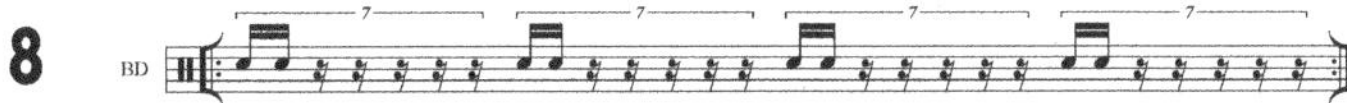

9

10

11

12

13

14

Incorporating a Syncopated Bass Drum Moving Melody

Groupings of "3" over a septuplet rate

Furthering your independence in varying your bass drum, the next step would be to incorporate variations of 16th note septuplet partials within an ongoing melody and then combing that with the current ostinato. The melody you will see in the next section is written as if were a snare melody, but you have the option of applying it to any limb that is applied to the kit. As with the previous exercises, we will be applying it to or playing it on the bass drum. An appropriate book to use which displays mixed partials in varied rate groupings is *Rhythm and Meter Patterns* by Gary Chaffee. The full melody in this section is an example of a page you may find in that book.

Below, find the example of the first 3 measures of the exercise (found on the next page) and how it is then applied to the bass drum under the current ostinato with groupings of "3" in a septuplet rate. Notice how you're seeing the first three measures only of the full melody exercise. Keep in mind that the groupings of "3" over the 16th note quintuplet rate will create 3 bar phrases total in order to come back to your starting point of beat 1. Below, find the process of assembling the bass drum melody with the ostinato.

Primary Ostinato

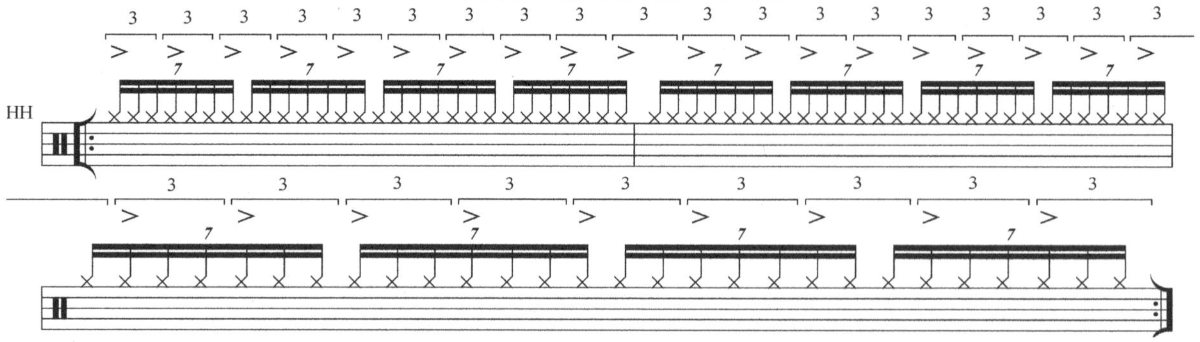

Bass Drum Melody (first three measures)

Combination (full phrase)

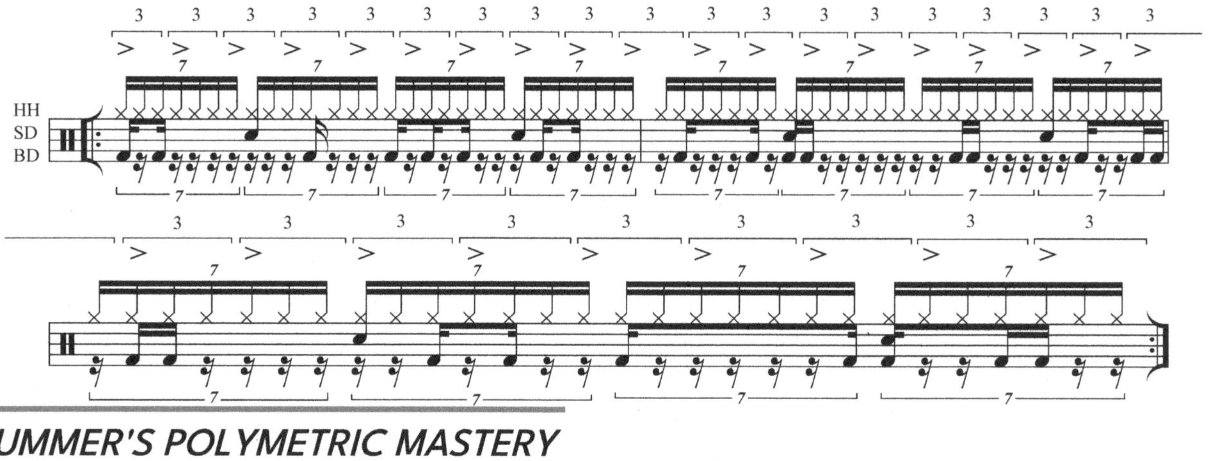

Exercise 42 : Syncopated Moving Melody with Septuplet Partials

16th note septuplet rate grooves with groupings of "3"

Below, you will find the transcription of the current ostinato once again. The rest of the page contains the entire rhythmic melody that will be applied to the bass drum. There are 3 ways you can go about working on these exercise pages for independence & variation development:

1) On a separate piece of paper, write out the ostinato 4 times. Insert the bass drum notes from the 12 measures of the melody below into the ostinato phrases you've transcribed.

2) Play down the whole exercise/melody and insert the accents (by ear) over the top of the exercise you are playing.

3) If you have a physical copy of the book, simply pencil in 16th note septuplets over the top of the melody and then write in accents in groupings of "3" over the ongoing septuplets.

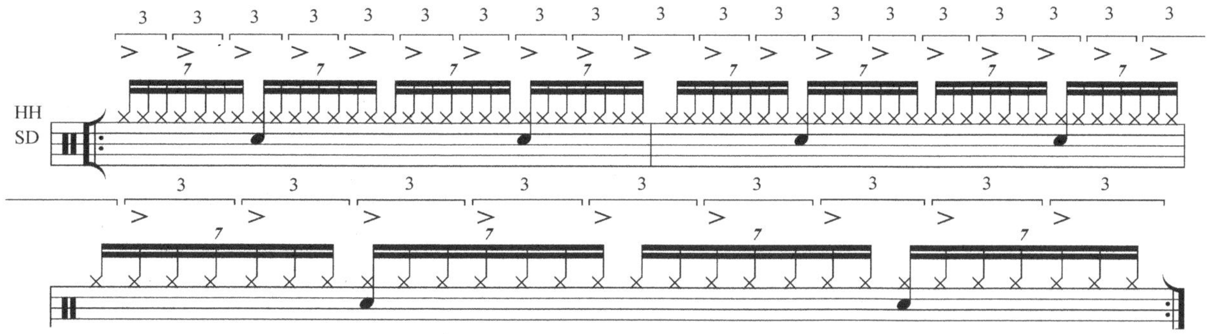

Asterisks designate the measures where the accented groupings & phrases of "3" will reset on beat 1 again

Section 10 : TUPLETS

Groupings of "4" over a 16th note septuplet rate in 4/4

In this portion of the book, the meter will still remain in 4/4. As in previous pages, this next section builds upon the current topics that have recently been explored. Continuing the topic of 'tuplets' in which the standard rate subdivision of each quarter note (of 2, 4, 8, etc....) expand into alternate choices (3, 5, 7, etc....), this segment of the book continues the topic of 16th note septuplets, or groupings beamed in 7 notes.

In a normal 4/4 meter comprising of consistent 16th note septuplets on the HH, it's safe to assume that one would eventually incorporate accents on downbeats to enhance the feel, sound and presence of the groove. The majority of drummers & instructors utilize and/or teach the usage of the Moeller technique to accurately execute the correct application of the accents. The breakdown of that HH pattern alone would look like this:

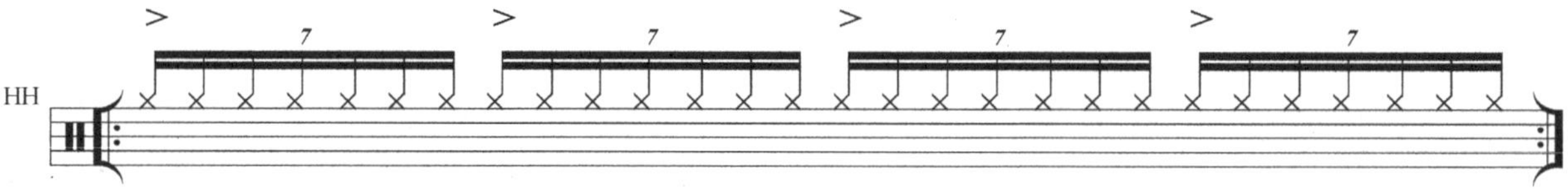

Adding the BD and SD in their proper places to create a "standard groove" with the septuplet rate, the complete pattern is the one seen here:

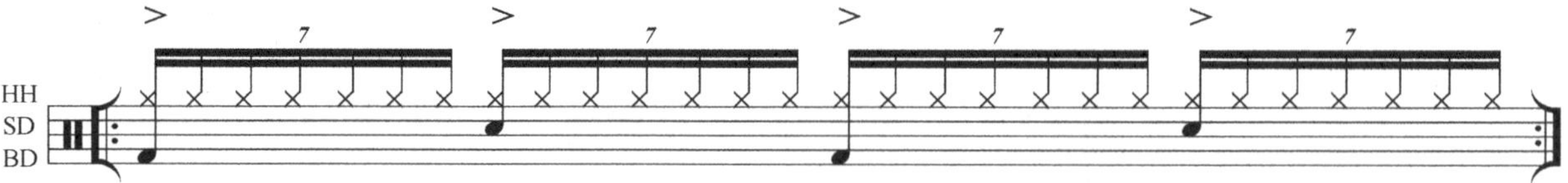

Notice that the above "standard groove" doesn't incorporate any cross rhythmic activity due to the accents laying on downbeats in the beamed groups of "7" and being in sync with the BD & SD pattern. However, in order to start displacing the accents and creating cross rhythmic ideas in a groove setting, a good place to start is to incorporate other numbered groupings in the time hand or limbs. Below is the breakdown of the same HH pattern but now utilizing groupings of "4" to create a cross rhythmic pattern. Take note that the groupings of "4" over a septuplet rate don't create an "over the bar" rhythm but it does create an "over the beat" rhythm (occurring in the space of every 2 quarter notes).

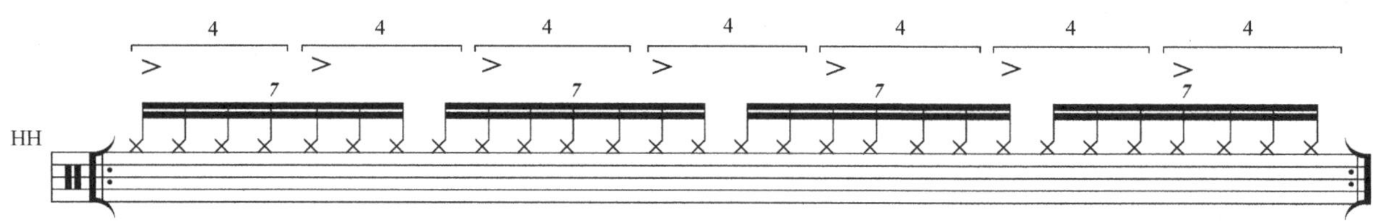

Tip: Counting Exercise

A good suggested exercise for any cross rhythm is to count out loud even before playing as to help build the two existing rhythms internally. Below, you will find a single measure phrase consisting of only 16th note septuplet note counts, but every 4th symbol is in **bold** as to represent the placement of an accent. There are several ways of counting septuplets. A popular method of counting is by using an Indian spoken syllable technique called Konnakol, applying the words "Ta Ka Di Mi Ta Ki Ta" as each syllabic count. Also, I often find a great method of counting odd-numbered grouping like septuplets is with a backwards count of "7654321." It allows for an evenly-spaced assortment of counts through each septuplet, though it may take some practice to obtain the flow of the syllables. However to start, let's keep it simple with a standardized method simply using "1234567" as your counts. Start by counting out loud, accentuating the bolded symbols while tapping your foot on downbeats in 4/4:

| **1** 2 3 4 **5** 6 7 | 2 **2** 3 4 5 **6** 7 | 3 2 **3** 4 5 6 **7** | 4 2 3 **4** 5 6 7 |

Primary Ostinato

The following pattern you see is the primary hand ostinato which will remain constant through the various grooves & exercises in this section. As your starting point, practice just this hand pattern together to develop independence involved in keeping the accents in groupings of "4" consistent over the top of the snare drum which remains on 2 & 4 throughout.

Practice Note: To obtain the most successful sound & feel of this ostinato, make sure that you are incorporating a repetitive 4-stroke Moeller accent technique in your time hand while you retain a consistent backbeat technique in the snare hand. Make an effort to ensure that the shifting accents do not affect or change the motion in either hand.

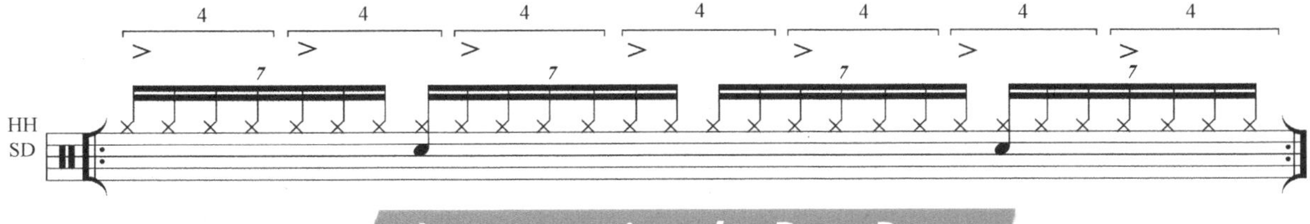

Incorporating the Bass Drum

The final goal is to now complete your phrases & grooves by adding countless bass drum rhythms to the ostinato. A great place to begin is to utilize the "partials," or each individual note of a 16th note septuplet grouping, one at a time, in your bass drum. Below is the basic septuplet groove with no accents followed by the same groove with the accents in groupings of "4" over the top in your time hand.

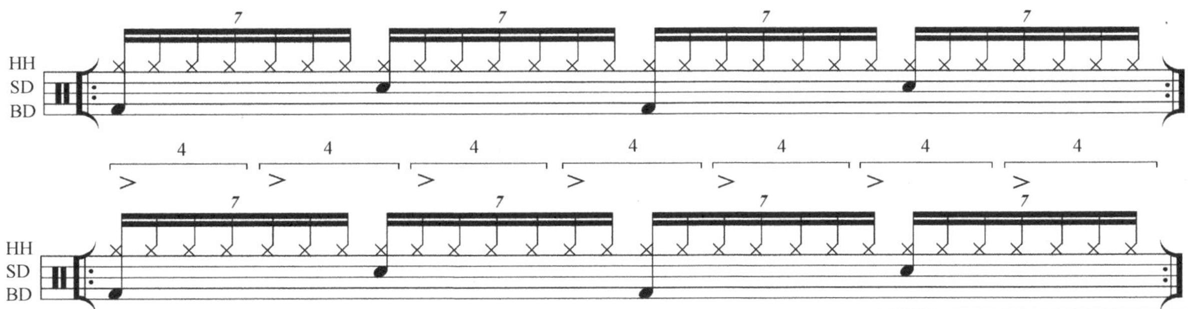

Exercise 43 : Septuplet Partials

Groupings of "4" over a 16th note septuplet rate with various BD partial combinations

Below, you will find the transcription of the current ostinato once again. The rest of the page contains partials, or "rhythmic portions," of the 16th note septuplet groupings for you to play in your bass drum. There are 3 ways you can go about working on these exercise pages for independence & variation development:

1) On a separate piece of paper, write out the ostinato 14 times. Extract 14 rhythms below and insert them one-by-one into the ostinato phrases you've transcribed as bass drum notes.

2) Play & repeat the one-measure ostinato and insert the rhythms below (by ear) into the hand pattern as bass drum notes.

3) If you have a physical copy of the book, simply pencil in a bass drum pattern from a single-measure rhythmic phrase into the ostinato. Once comfortable, erase and then move to transcribing the next rhythms down the page one-by-one.

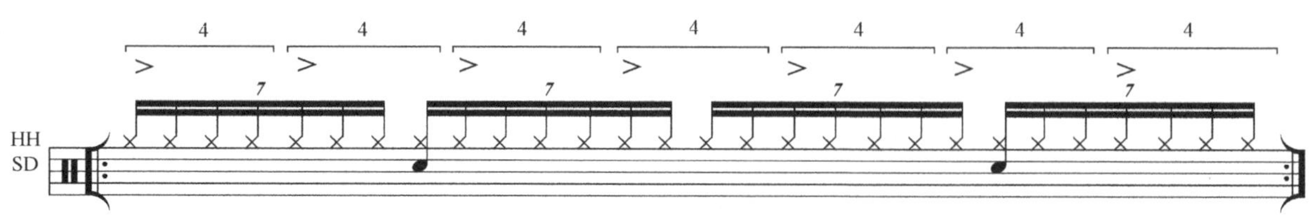

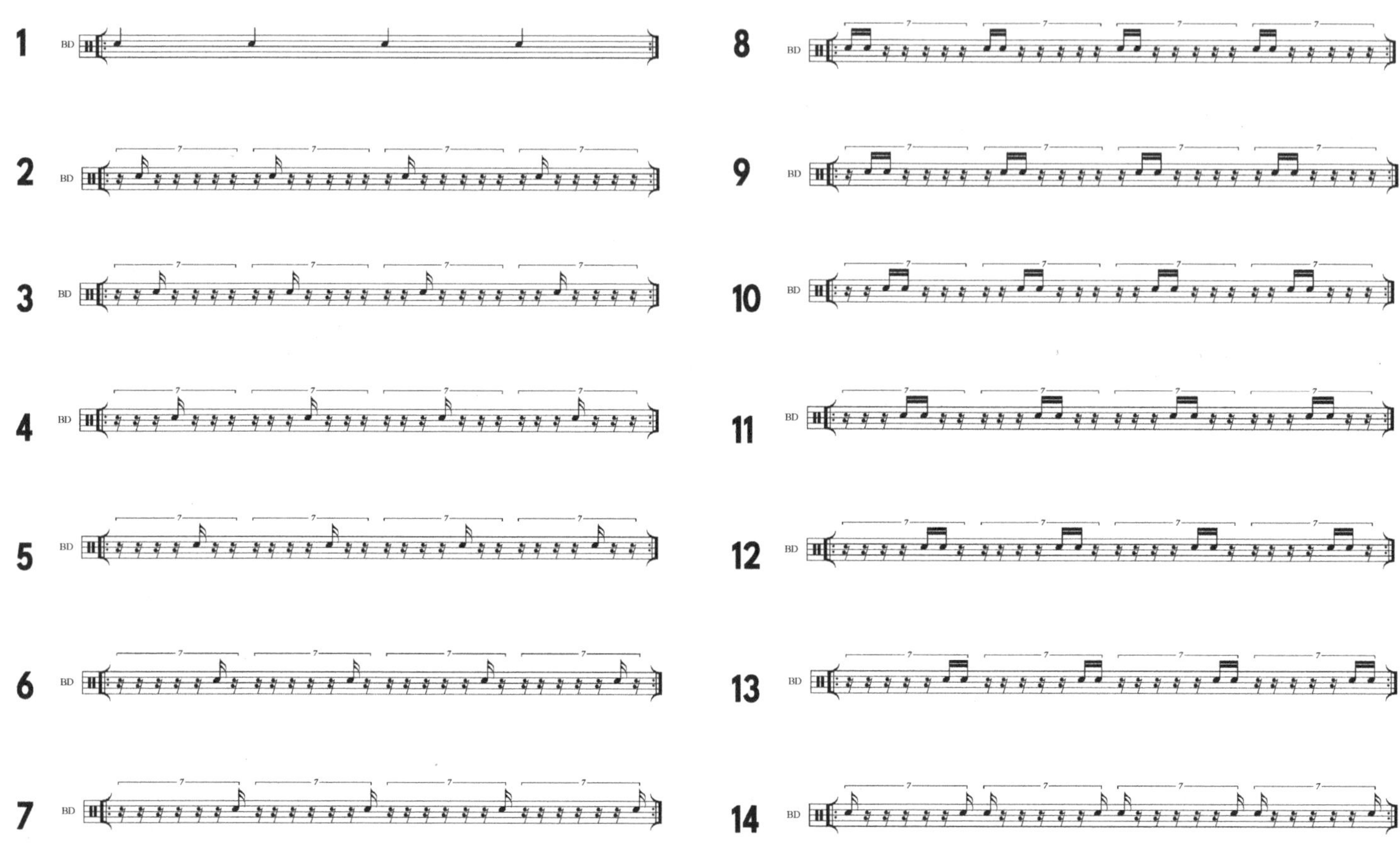

Incorporating a Syncopated Bass Drum Moving Melody

Groupings of "4" over a septuplet rate

Furthering your independence in varying your bass drum, the next step would be to incorporate variations of 16th note septuplet partials within an ongoing melody and then combing that with the current ostinato. The melody you will see in the next section is written as if were a snare melody, but you have the option of applying it to any limb that is applied to the kit. As with the previous exercises, we will be applying it to or playing it on the bass drum. An appropriate book to use which displays mixed partials in varied rate groupings is 'Rhythm and Meter Patterns' by Gary Chaffee. The full melody in this section is an example of a page you may find in that book.

Below, find the example of the first measure of the exercise (found on the next page) and how it is then applied to the bass drum under the current ostinato with groupings of "4" in a septuplet rate. Notice how you're seeing the first measure only of the full melody exercise. Keep in mind that, as with the groupings of "2" over the septuplet rate, the groupings of "4" only span the length of 1 measure total and reset on the downbeat of each measure. Below, find the process of assembling the bass drum melody with the ostinato

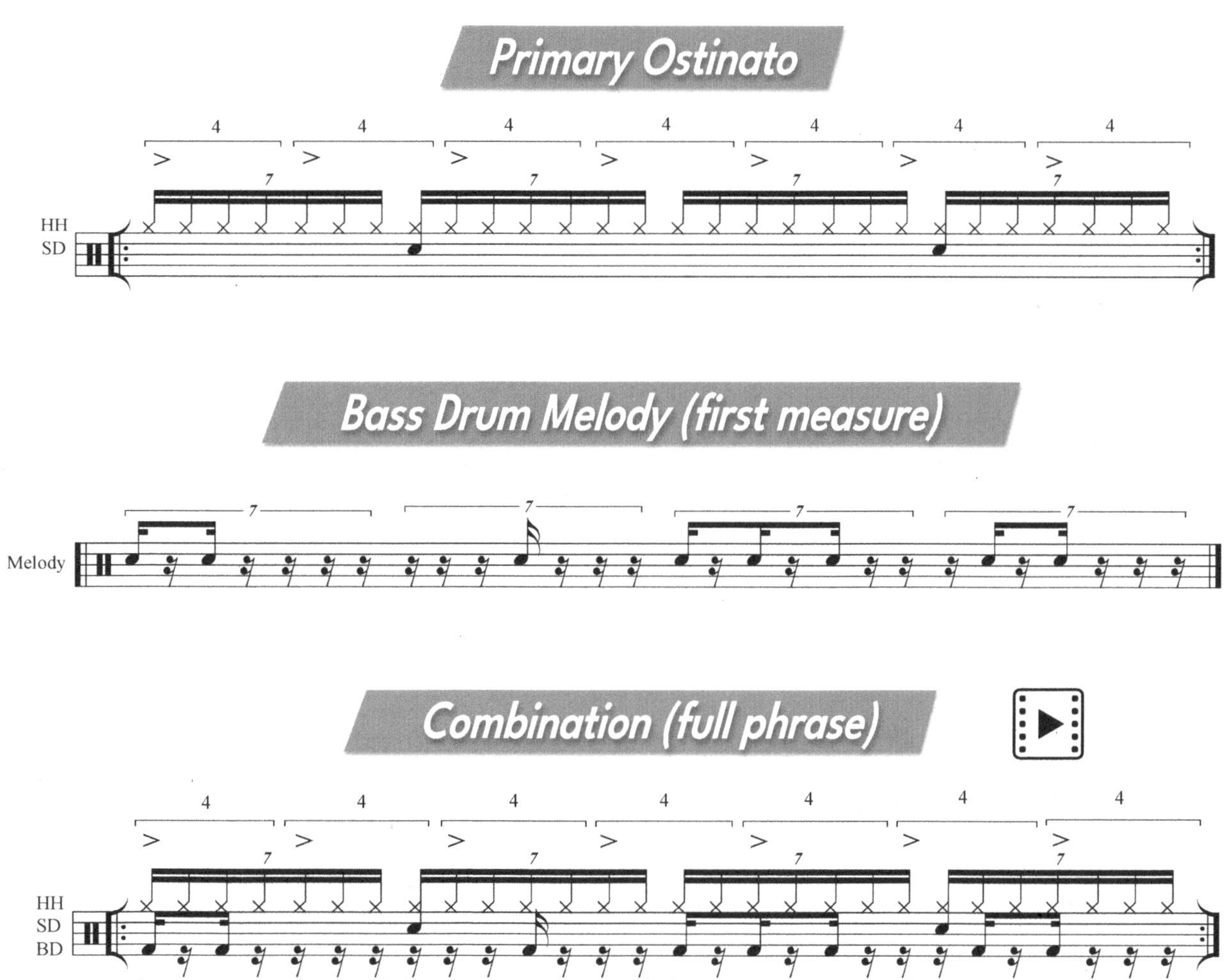

Exercise 44 : Syncopated Moving Melody with Septuplet Partials

16th note septuplet rate grooves with groupings of “4”

Below, you will find the transcription of the current ostinato once again. The rest of the page contains the entire rhythmic melody that will be applied to the bass drum. There are 3 ways you can go about working on these exercise pages for independence & variation development:

1) On a separate piece of paper, write out the ostinato 12 times. Insert the bass drum notes from the 12 measures of the melody below into the ostinato phrases you’ve transcribed.

2) Play down the whole exercise/melody and insert the accents (by ear) over the top of the exercise you are playing.

3) If you have a physical copy of the book, simply pencil in 16th note septuplets over the top of the melody and then write in accents in groupings of “4” over the ongoing septuplets.

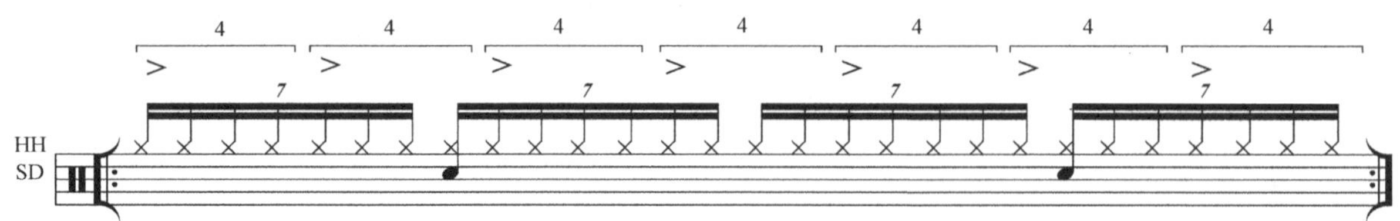

Melody

NOTES

ACKNOWLEDGMENTS

Jason Gianni would gladly like to thank:

Joe Bergamini, Rob Wallis and everyone at Hudson Music, the amazing & talented Terry Branam, Greg Crane, Daryl Anderson, John Whittman, Prudence Elliot, Jim Haler, Jalissa Gascho, Dave Gerhart, Chris Dolson, Matt Rudin, Joel Tetzlaff, Jeff Shipley and everyone at YAMAHA Drums, Kelly Paiste, Jacqueline Paiste, Erik Paiste, Tim Shahady, Javier Caudillo, Julie Bao, April Mendoza and everyone at PAISTE Cymbals, Bruce Jacoby, Roger Johnson, Chris Hart and everyone at REMO Inc., Joe Testa, Brian Stockton and everyone at VIC FIRTH, Mike Berg, Lucian Pop, Mark Allee, Phil Trocchio and everyone at HUMES & BERG, Jason Edwards at PROLOGIX PERCUSSION, Tony Maggiolino, Yukari Nakagawa, Fernando Hernandez, Steve Marks, Chris Biesterfeldt, Bob Quaranta and everyone at The Collective NYC, Anthony Citrinite, John Castellano, Peter Retzlaff, Ian Froman, Adriano Santos, Chris Coleman, Camille Gainer, John Longstreth, Fred Klatz, Jim Mola, Vince Cherico, Dave Previ, Maciek Shecjbal, Tobias Ralph, Marko Drordjevic, Leroy Clouden, Mark Flynn, Pat Petrillo, Yoichi Sato, Liberty DeVito, the late Frank Katz & Kim Plainfield and every brilliant instructor I shared so many years with at The Drummers Collective, Mark Powers, Eric C. Hughes, Joshua Simonds, Dave Stanoch and everyone at PASIC, Alex "boy scout" Cohen, Dave Elitch, Jonathan Mover, Dena Tauriello, Sammy Merendino, Jon Weber, Harvey Price, Tom Palmer, Dan Armstrong, Glenn Weber, Dan, Nja and Steven Shinder at Drum Talk TV, Joe Deninzon, Michelangelo Quirinale, Bill Hubauer and everyone with Stratospheerius, Cheri Martorana, Scott Lovelady, John LaSpina and the whole Rubix Kube family, Mark Wood, Laura Kaye, Deb Wyant, Rob Bambach, Paul Ranieri, Matt Vanacoro and the whole MWROC family, Tony DeLauro, Hal Seltzer and everyone at the Rock of Ages Broadway Band, Geno Amato and everyone at The Royal Scam, Ed Palermo and everyone at The Ed Palermo Big Band, Quinn Lemley and everyone at The Ultimate Queen Celebration, Phil Ehart, Tom Brislin, Eric Holmquist and everyone in Kansas, my previous University of the Arts family, my New School family, everyone at Modern Drummer, Chaz Bufe of See Sharp Press, Mick Berry, and everyone else that has had such an amazing impact on my life as a musician. You are in my thoughts and praises every day!

A very special thank you and debt of gratitude to Steve Smith, Mike Mangini, Thomas Lang and especially David Garibaldi for their invaluable & significant contributions. The music notes on these pages represent countless years of influence from your remarkable minds to my life & career as a musician.

I would especially like to thank my extended family as well as my immediate family: Dale and Richard Gianni, Lisa, Josh and Harper Aaron, Ronni and Rick Levine, and most of all, the two people that complete the two halves of my heart to become whole, Jody and Bella Gianni. I love you all more than you'll ever know!